This is the Christian life in reality—the pain of living in a fallen world where the innocent often suffer, the joy of knowing Jesus, and the wonder and mystery of faith in a God who can, and sometimes does intervene in a miraculous way! Here is not a naive, 'plastic' story with a 'fairy-tale' end. There are tears, doubts, anger and, at times, total confusion about what God is doing.

This book will help many who are going through heartache, for those who look on helplessly when loved ones, particularly children, are suffering and there seems no answer from God.

The story has a happy ending, but for those who have not yet received such an answer, and perhaps in this life never will, it shows a way through the pain and doubt, not to avoid it, but to survive and still trust in the Lord!

Roger Jones
Christian Music Ministries

I'LL GIVE YOU BACK A HEALTHY CHILD

Eleanor Hall

Christian Focus Publications

All royalties will be shared between the Birmingham Children's Hospital and the Glasgow Royal Sick Children's Hospital.

© 1994 Eleanor Hall
ISBN 1-85792-110-0

Published by
Christian Focus Publications Ltd
Geanies House, Fearn, Ross-shire
IV20 1TW, Scotland, Great Britain.

Cover design by Donna Macleod

Printed and bound in Great Britain
by Cox & Wyman Ltd, Reading, Berkshire

The song 'Time to fly' is © 1988 Word Music UK

Unless otherwise stated, Scripture quotations are from the
New International Version,
published by Hodder & Stoughton.

Contents

1. Foreword by Janet Gaukroger 8

1. FROM BIRTH TO BIRMINGHAM 11

2. SETTLING DOWN 22

3. OUT OF CONTROL 34

4. INTENSIVE CARE AGAIN 49

5. I'LL GIVE YOU BACK A HEALTHY CHILD 67

6. A DIAGNOSIS 72

7. BACK TO BIRMINGHAM 76

8. BRAIN SURGERY 86

9. THEATRE AGAIN 99

10. HOPE THROUGH DESPAIR 107

11. ANOTHER CHANCE 126

12. RECOVERING AT HOME 139

13. STATIONING 152

14. EPILOGUE 165

ACKNOWLEDGEMENTS

I would like to thank staff from the various departments of the Children's Hospital in Birmingham involved in caring for our son.

A special thanks to Dr Rylance and his team and to his secretaries for allowing me to invade the privacy of their office whilst researching this book.

We are grateful to Mr Walsh and the neurosurgical team and to Professor Stephenson at the Sick Children's Hospital in Glasgow. Also many thanks to Dr R. Duncan, registrar in neurology at the Southern General Hospital in Glasgow.

Our appreciation to our parents for all their support and for the love shown by family and friends.

We are indebted to the community at Queen's College for helping us during our time of need.

Thank you to my husband for encouraging me to complete this book. He never showed his boredom when forced to listen to countless excerpts from the manuscript.

FOREWORD

The Bible is full of real stories about real things that happened to real people. How encouraging it is to know that we are not the only ones who struggle with circumstances in our lives!

Eleanor Hall's story is a real one, too. With honesty she shares the heartbreak and agony of her youngest son's illness. Although her deep, strong faith in God is never in doubt, she openly shares the difficult and searching questions she asked of Him in the darkest hours.

As Christians we say that God's Word is a lamp for our feet and a light to guide our path. This was certainly the case for Eleanor as, time and time again, she found comfort and hope in the pages of what must be a very well-worn Bible!

Through the stories of God's people in the Old and New Testaments, and through the pages of church history, we know that God is always faithful in meeting the needs of His children. Yet, it is inspiring to keep on hearing new accounts of God's provision for those who love Him.

I was very moved as I read this story. I found myself laughing with the Halls on a few occasions, and certainly crying with them at others. As a mother, I felt very deeply the anguish of the thought of losing a child. As one involved in church ministry I was warmed by the generous practical and spiritual support shown to the family by their Christian friends.

Corrie ten Boom, a well-known Christian who was imprisoned during World War II for hiding Jews in her home, often shared the words her sister said to her in the most difficult times in the concentration camp: 'There is no pit that God is not deeper yet'. Eleanor Hall's story is testimony to that.

I pray that as you read this book you will be strengthened in your understanding of the width, length, height and depth of the love of God. I pray, too, that whatever the difficult circumstances of your life, you will know more and more the reality of His sustaining power. However deep the pit may seem, God is indeed deeper yet!

Janet Gaukroger

CHAPTER 1

FROM BIRTH TO BIRMINGHAM
(August 1989-August 1991)

We had taken our children to a country park, near to our home in Uddingston (Glasgow). As we passed the stork pen I walked over, peeped through the mesh and called, 'Pst, boys, the next time you're flying over Viewpark, don't stop, just keep flying, we're happy now with four children!' And indeed we were. John James Hall's arrival on 16/4/90 seemed to complete our family of two girls and two boys.

His conception had come quite unexpectedly - *quite unexpectedly*! It wasn't that we didn't want another baby, it was the timing that concerned us. My husband Dave, who worked as a self-employed joiner, was in the process of candidating for the Methodist ministry. If he was accepted, it would entail us having to move to college down south, away from family and friends. I had happily given up my nursing career to look after our three children; Caroline aged four, Louise aged two, and David, our eight month old baby son. But faced with the prospect of being pulled away from my roots to set up home in an unfamiliar environment, I could only wonder how I was going to cope with three young children and a new baby.

Before the pregnancy was confirmed, I came across

a verse of scripture which left me rooted to the chair in disbelief, with my mouth hanging open rather longer than would be considered elegant for a lady! I had picked up the Bible with the intention of reading I Timothy, but to my surprise it opened at Jeremiah 8. My eyes fell on verse 7 which seemed to stand out: *even the stork in the heavens knows her times* (RSV). It was the word 'stork,' - stork, the symbol of deliveries. I knew from that moment onwards I was pregnant.

The pregnancy had gone quite well with all the normal symptoms of tiredness, nausea and notions. But one little hitch had worried me. I was bitten by a dog during the second trimester and, although the skin was only slightly broken, I felt it important to inform my GP. After checking with the local maternity hospital he advised a tetanus injection, just to be on the safe side. Despite being reassured, I remember feeling reluctant about having it, wondering if it would in some way harm the baby. I had the first injection but decided against having the remaining two required to complete the course. Other than gaining very little weight the remainder of the pregnancy was uneventful.

On Easter Sunday, 1990, my labour pains began. By midnight they were becoming more frequent. As I lay in bed timing contractions, I decided, in order to take my mind off things, to resume where I'd left off reading in the Psalms. (As if I could!) Prior to this I had been pondering over my present labour and subsequent delivery. Routinely when the sac of fluid containing the baby ruptures (this is known in layman's terms as 'waters breaking'), mothers are taken straight to the labour ward for the imminent delivery of the baby. My thoughts had been concentrated on the 'waters breaking' side of things when to my surprise, on opening the Bible at Psalm 69:1, the following words appeared, 'Save me, O God, for the waters have come up to my neck!' My burst of laughter woke up Dave, who had been dozing beside me. He was curious to find out what was so funny? Who would believe I could come across a verse so out of context, and yet so appropriate?

It was ironic to think that for the first four years of our marriage we'd prayed desperately for a family and now here I was cradling our fourth child.

Interview

Dave was accepted for training with the Methodist Church and given a place at Hartley Victoria College in Manchester. So with John only a fortnight old we set off to meet the Principal. We were also to look at the house that had been allocated to us. It was a ten minute drive from the college.

I remember on arriving in Manchester, that we stopped at a garage for petrol. As Dave filled up I was left for a few minutes, alone with John and my thoughts. Tears rolled down my cheeks as I prayed, 'Lord, I can't face leaving home and moving down from Scotland. My life is so settled there.' Nothing seemed to feel right except for one thing - we both had the same conviction that the Lord had called Dave into the ordained ministry.

The interview went well and the people we met were friendly and helpful. To begin with, I had no intentions of entering into the spirit of things, preferring to remain polite but most certainly detached. That was until the Principal and his wife broached the subject of our domestic situation. They reminded us of the option to defer for one year until our family was at a more manageable age. 'Now this is more like it,' I thought, 'a couple after my own heart! The pressure off, I could relax. Who knows, the move might never materialise.' We agreed to be deferred for one year.

John developed well over the next few months, reaching all his milestones within the accepted time although a little later than his siblings. He was breast fed for the first eleven months and was an extremely healthy baby. One feature was his mop of thick dark hair which always seemed to stick up, Mohican style! He had long dark eyelashes which were the envy of most women who met him and a deep loud voice which sounded extraordinary in a child of his age.

The last few months at home were confused, tearful months for me, with my heart not in our plans. It seemed that all we stood for as Christians was being put to the test, as we accepted the call to the ministry. At times I wondered if the Lord was only proving our obedience, faithfulness and love for Him. Maybe if we showed a *willingness* to go, then that would be all that would be required of us. Some days were agony, almost suffocating, especially as the time to leave approached; the pressure of not wanting to go, but knowing I must was unbearable. Even on the very last day, as we pulled away from our home, I would readily have turned back, had the Lord so guided, and would have counted it a pleasure to empty the removal van single-handed!

God's confirmation

One night as we were praying together I had a message in 'tongues'. We sat quietly for a few moments before the Holy Spirit revealed the interpretation to Dave; 'As the leopard leaps and bounds I go on ahead to prepare the way for you.' As the words poured forth from Dave's mouth I could visualise the beast in all its beauty pounding along through hills and forests, then resting and looking round to see if we were following.

This message was confirmed not long after by a minister at the close of an evening service. When he was pronouncing the blessing he said, 'Lord, You don't send us on, then follow, but You go on ahead of us.' I could hardly believe what I'd just heard. It was not typical of the blessings offered and it was almost identical to Dave's interpretation. The Lord was speaking to us through these words. As well as confirming Dave's 'call' to the ordained ministry, we were being assured of Christ's love and presence with us and that He had a special plan for our lives. My tears subsided and the comfort I felt helped me over the following weeks as we slowly prepared to leave our home.

Two verses of scripture also spoke strongly to me. One was Matthew 8:20: 'Foxes have holes and birds of the air have nests but the Son of Man has no place to lay his head.' I realised that for the rest of our lives we would be a little like nomads moving from church to church and never really having a place to call our own. It was a lifestyle I had never envisaged and would certainly never have chosen.

The other verse was Matthew 19:29: 'And everyone

who has left houses or brothers or sisters or father or mother or children or fields for my sake will receive a hundred times as much and will inherit eternal life.' For me the hardest part of all was leaving parents, family and friends. At times I couldn't bear the thought of the separation and dreaded the day when we would finally have to move.

My parents, both retired, lived only a few streets away and simply adored their grandchildren. They were always available to help with the children and, with us having four under school age, were a God-send on many a day. Not only were they parents and grandparents but they were our friends. How were they going to manage when we had gone? Were we not emptying their world by taking their grandchildren away from them? I finally had to surrender them into the Lord's care, and trust Him to fill the void when we were gone. In so doing a burden was lifted, giving me the assurance that they were in safe and caring hands.

Although Dave's parents and family lived in New-castle, where he was born and raised, the distance hadn't prevented us from visiting each other regularly. In fact, after we became parents we made a special effort to see them as we did not want our children to miss out on the unique love that grandparents give so freely. If the college had been nearer to them it would have been one consolation, but by going south we were actually going to be a little further away.

The year had come and gone much too quickly for my liking. Before we knew it, we were counting the weeks before Dave was due to start college. Everything had

16

remained exactly as planned until we received a call from the Principal at Manchester offering us a place at Queen's College in Birmingham. A four bedroomed flat had become vacant on the campus there. We accepted, as living in a community, with Dave on hand most of the time, would no doubt make life easier for me. We visited the college and were happy with the flat and the surroundings. Term times were similar to Manchester where we were scheduled to start in September, 1991.

Unexpected trouble

Three weeks before we were due to leave we suffered a tremendous shock, when John, our healthy little sixteen month old boy, suffered his first convulsion. This occurred five days after his MMR injection,* so naturally we presumed there was some connection.

We had been invited to visit friends in Edinburgh. Because little David was a bit off colour my mother suggested leaving the boys with her, and taking the girls with us. As we pulled up outside our friends' home they were waiting with news that they had received a phone call from my mother to say David was quite unwell. I returned the call to find my mother sounding desperate over the phone.

'He's shaking all over and his temperature seems high.'

'I'm puzzled, Mam,' I said, 'David seemed alright when we left.'

'It's not David,' she replied, 'It's John!'

---

*details of medical terms are in a glossary at the end of the book

17

I knew straightaway he was having a febrile convulsion but couldn't understand why, as he hadn't shown signs of any illness that day.

By the time we got home he was already into his second fit. Whilst my brother and his wife threw water on John in an effort to cool him down and bring him round, my mother was pacing the floor like someone deranged. Although my years of nursing experience had involved dealing with people having seizures, it was heartbreaking to witness my own son twitching and jerking uncontrollably, not conscious of his surroundings. As I held him in my arms he appeared the size of a six month old baby; his little face seemed so small and his frame so helpless.

We rushed him to hospital where he was admitted for four days. During this time he took a further two fits. Although he eventually settled, he was very unsteady on his feet. We did not know whether or not this unsteadiness was due to the convulsions because John had only been walking for a few weeks and, like all children learning to walk, was constantly losing his balance.

On discharge the consultant explained that this might be a one-off experience for John. He added that it was probably due to John's high temperature caused by an ear infection. On the other hand some children go on to develop epilepsy. Only time would tell. We hoped the former would be true for John and we could put it all behind us. We were given medication to keep at home and instructed to use it only in an emergency situation if he developed a prolonged fit.

Farewell to Glasgow

Before we left for college, we were given a farewell evening and presentation by friends from the Methodist Church where Dave was a local preacher. Although the service was both moving and inspiring, it was a very tearful evening for me. In fact I cried all the way through the service and was still crying as they were washing up the cups at the close of the evening! Guess it was obvious that I was not keen to go!

Another farewell celebration had been organised at the local Church of Scotland where I'd worshipped since childhood. There we had been blessed with many friends - friendships that had stood the test of time. We were touched by the presence of those who had made a special effort to join us, due to distance or disability.

It, too, was a very emotional evening, but with an additional reason this time - I had reached the big 4-0- and unfortunately they had not forgotten! Before my eyes, a banner stretched across the room, bearing the words: CONGRATULATIONS! FORTY TODAY! How could they do this? How could they expose me? All over the place balloons, that bobbed and bounced, bore slogans that accurately reflected my pain: OH NO 4-0! When the candles on the birthday cake were lit I feared the 'sprinklers' would automatically switch on in response to the heat!

The balloons were left in the car after the party which had taken place two days before we left for Birmingham. I took care to burst them before we reached Queen's College and prayed the children would not give me away.

They say that life begins at 40. They lied! My dark hair was being replaced by grey at a phenomenal rate; the anti-wrinkle cream, however thickly or however often applied, didn't work; my eyes could only focus when the page was held at a distance; and when I stopped in the middle of a conversation it wasn't to find the most appropriate word, but to remember what I was talking about in the first place! So if this was life beginning, then I was dreading middle age!

It was a wonderful time and we appreciated the many cards, gifts and well-wishes. We shall never forget the thoughtfulness, kindness and love shown to us that evening which made it a 'send-off' in a million. Our friends had put in a lot of hard work in arranging it. We were so grateful for this and for the way in which they constantly sought out anything of interest that might help ease the tension of the pending move.

An example of this came from a close friend, Aileen, who had found a song on a demo-tape of Christian music which had appealed to her. She felt sure we would be able to identify fully with the lyrics. She wasn't wrong. It was as though the song had been written especially for us because the words were very apt for our situation. In a strange kind of way, they comforted and served once again to reinforce Dave's call to the ordained ministry. The song, which had a beautiful melody, was written by Chris Christensen and recorded by *The Christensens*.

TIME TO FLY

Like the birds we must someday leave the nest,
And put what we've been learning to the test,

We should not shrink back or be afraid to fall,
When we hear His voice, the upward call.

CHORUS
It's time to fly, it's time to spread our wings and catch
the wind of the Spirit, it's blowing through our lives,
And it's time to soar higher than we've been before
The wind of the Spirit is blowing, is blowing through
our lives.

Seasons change there's something stirring in the air,
We're seeing signs and wonders everywhere,
Old men dream dreams, our children prophesy,
And just obey His voice and don't ask why.

We will go wherever that strong wind will blow,
Where each of us will land, we do not know,
Oh but we will fly together under His command,
We know our destinies are in His hand.

The song stirred a strange kind of excitement within me. Yet there were days when I often felt like a little bird being 'pushed' from the nest instead of being allowed to 'fly' freely. I strongly resented the idea! But the more we played the song, the more we were convinced that we had made the right decision. Nevertheless at times the love the little 'sparrow' had for the cosy nest outweighed the challenge of the future flight. Even on the day we left, I still hoped the Lord would stop us in our tracks and allow us to stay.

We arrived at Queen's College on the last day of August, 1991 at 4.30 pm!

CHAPTER 2

SETTLING DOWN
(September 1991-February 1992)

The first few weeks were hectic as we settled into college life and found our way around, but we managed eventually to get ourselves organised.

The children enjoyed exploring the grounds and soon made friends with the other children who were also finding their feet. Louise started school a couple of days after we arrived and Caroline a few weeks later following an appeal. We managed to find David a place in a local playgroup three mornings a week whilst John stayed at home quite happily with me. Before we knew it term had started and Dave was enjoying life as a student minister.

Unfortunately the whole family was plagued with constant illness and mishaps so it didn't take us long to clock up 6 gastric flu's, 5 throat viruses, 4 bouts of chicken pox, 3 cases of croup, 2 painful ears, 1 melted telly and a partridge in a pear tree!

I'm sure our new GP must have had second thoughts about us. We registered with him in September and had called him out several times during the first few weeks. He was leading a patient into his office one day when he bumped into us. He said, 'Robert, meet the Hall family' in such a manner as to suggest we spelt *trouble*!

John taken to hospital

Around midnight, only a few weeks after we'd arrived at Queen's, we heard an almighty piercing scream. We ran to John's cot to find him in a grand mal fit. Dave rushed downstairs to our neighbour's house to collect the medication, (we'd left it in their fridge the day we'd arrived and had forgotten to get it back). Meanwhile, I stayed with John. As I watched, he stopped breathing, and his colour changed from blue to grey. I grabbed him from his cot, cradled him in my arms and screamed at the top of my voice, 'Jesus, help me!'

Louise came running through to see what all the commotion was about. She was so frightened by the expression on my face and the fear in my voice that she made a hasty retreat back to her bed without a word. Caroline had been woken by the screams but had lain too terrified to move as she could sense something was seriously wrong.

I raced with John in my arms to the phone and dialled 999 but left the receiver dangling in sheer shock and panic. Like someone deranged I ran to the front door and screamed, as I knelt down with John, 'Dave, hurry! We're losing him!'

Our neighbour, a physiotherapist, arrived with Dave and told me later that she thought John had died and she would have to give him mouth-to-mouth resuscitation. Fortunately after Dave gave John the medication rectally he started to breathe and his colour improved. I raced back to the phone and dialled 999 to summon an ambulance.

John was taken to the Casualty Department of the Children's Hospital. The staff were wonderful to both

John and to ourselves. Dr Plant, one of the Senior Registrars, took time to listen and to advise us and was both sympathetic and supportive when I 'broke down'.

Due to a shortage of beds, John was admitted to Ward 9, the Infectious Disease Ward. There over the next few days he had another few fits. Various tests were run (e.g. lumbar puncture, EEG, CT Scan and blood tests) but they all proved negative. Initially John's temperature was difficult to control but eventually it settled. A week later he was discharged with the same diagnosis as we'd been given in Scotland.

It was now October. His balance was much worse after the convulsions, and although it eventually improved, he still had a slight degree of unsteadiness.

By November we were still trying to find our feet and establish some kind of routine, when John started fitting again and had to be taken to hospital. It was early in the morning and we were extremely anxious and exhausted. The Senior House Officer on call examined John carefully, then suggested that we take him home and bring him back in the morning to see the consultant, Dr Rylance. He had to confirm this with the Registrar, and left the room for a few minutes. When we overheard him say on the phone that 'The parents are ultra-sensible people!', we both looked at each other and burst out laughing. We were so ultra-sensible that only a day or so before, Dave had put John in his high chair and had then gone to look for him!

The consultant confirmed our suspicion that John had a tendency towards epilepsy. A pattern seemed to be emerging of four fits every four to six weeks. I remember feeling completely stunned at this diagnosis. John, an epileptic? Surely not. No doubt most parents have a similar reaction when their precious child is given a medical label for the first time, be it diabetic, asthmatic, epileptic or whatever. It takes a while to sink in. Dr Rylance advised medication but suggested we talk it over and let him know our decision at the next out-patient appointment. This we were happy to do and took John home.

Before John was discharged Mickey Mouse visited the ward along with the Lord Mayor of Birmingham to promote a forthcoming ice show. The children were filled with awe and delighted to receive Mickey Mouse hats complete with ears! John was ecstatic and screamed, 'Mouse, Mouse!' Later a journalist returned and asked if John could be photographed for the evening newspaper. It was a pleasure to see the wonder on his face, and as the Lord Mayor held him he carried out their request to pull Mickey's nose for the photograph. I don't know who was cheered the most that day, John or me. It was a wonderful send-off; we were going home, and for the present that was all that mattered.

We talked and prayed about John's future and decided to wait (probably in the hope that the problem would miraculously disappear). If the fits should return, there would be no option but to allow the introduction of anti-convulsants. On one particular evening I had tossed the options in my mind and concluded that I would hate John to have to depend on drugs. The following morning, however, the first words that entered my mind were, 'John is going to need medication.'

I felt that the Lord was speaking but I could not understand why. Not wanting to believe it I wondered whether it was just my imagination or the enemy at work. Only time would tell. Surely the Lord can heal John divinely if He chooses, I thought. James 5: 14, 15 kept coming into my mind: Is any one of you sick? He should call the elders of the church to pray over him and anoint him with oil in the name of the Lord. And the prayer offered in faith will make the sick person well; the Lord will raise him up.

Prayers for healing

Dave and I decided to step out in faith and ask the Principal of the college, The Rev Dr J Walker, along with a few tutors and students, to pray with John and anoint him with oil. It was decided for John's sake to keep this as informal and natural as possible. So with John playing on the floor of our living-room, surrounded by friends and family, he was gently anointed with oil and a prayer made to the Lord for his healing. He seemed to sense something special was happening as he remained quiet and co-operative throughout. The Principal also felt it important to minister to us as a family. So those present gathered round and, placing their hands upon us, prayed that we would receive both help and the strength to cope.

It was a very moving time and we were grateful for the love and support we received. Obviously the only way we would know if John had been healed would be the absence of any further fits. But also, the evidence of his total healing would be realised when he was able to walk without losing his balance, something he'd never been capable of before.

John continued to grow and develop speech and social skills. He was such a loving child and had a pleasant disposition. His thick dark hair, his deep voice and his outgoing personality made him quite a character. In the college dining-room he would sit in the high chair and call at the top of his voice to each of the students as they came into the room. They had no option but to take notice as he would continue to call their names until they responded; and with a voice as loud as John's one had to take notice! But still his balance was poor.

We were sure our children had settled well into college life and were unaware of any unhappiness or homesickness. Therefore when young David started 'playing up' during a meal one evening, we were taken aback. It was so out of character for him as he was normally such a good-natured child. Because of the embarrassment he was causing, I wanted to run him out of the dining-room by the scruff of the neck, but I managed, just, to keep my cool. When I had him alone I asked what was wrong. He looked up with the saddest blue eyes and said, 'I don't know.' I believed him, and knew this was not a time for discipline. I gathered him in my arms and held him tightly to me until he calmed down.

Later, in the chapel he started all over again. My patience was growing thin and I felt like shaking him. I wondered if the attention his brother had been getting was provoking some kind of jealousy. But when I asked him again to tell me what was wrong I was taken aback at his reply. The expression on his face revealed his pain and confusion. 'I want my old house.' 'His old house? Oh bless him, I thought, he's homesick.'

We had been more concerned about the girls feeling this way since they were a little older and at an age to understand. But David was just over two-and-a-half when we moved, so we didn't think it would have affected him at all. Later we learned that around the three year old mark had been the worst age for other children whose parents had moved from home to the campus; some had actually regressed and started bed-wetting.

Not long after, the words I'd heard so vividly, 'John is going to need medication' came to fruition. He had to be admitted to hospital and commenced on anti-convulsant therapy to control a further episode of seizures. It would be easy to think that the prayers and anointing with oil had been a waste of time. We truly did not believe so. Now we know that precious afternoon was a preparation, both spiritually and physically, for John, our children and ourselves to face the months ahead.

The wise men came bearing gifts from afar, but a few days before Christmas little David came bearing chickenpox spots from the playgroup! The incubation period unfolded textbook style so by the turn of the year, as the spots were disappearing from David's skin, they were bursting forth in varying degrees on our other three children. John caught a really bad dose of the virus which unfortunately set him fitting again and into the Infectious Disease Ward at the Children's Hospital. Whilst on the ward, he had a prolonged fit which lasted over half-an-hour and left me totally petrified.

The main problem for the medical staff was finding access to inject intravenously the anti-convulsant because there was hardly an area of skin free from blisters and scabs. As they made one attempt after another I began to panic inside as I knew it wouldn't be doing John any good to fit for this length of time.

Eventually the Sister in charge showed me to her office and then phoned Dave to put him in the picture. I was frightened and physically trembling when I asked if she could contact the Hospital Chaplain as well. It was during this time of waiting in the office that my eye caught the following poem pinned on the wall.

DON'T QUIT

When things go wrong as they sometimes will;
when the road you're trudging seems all uphill;
when the funds are low and debts are high
and you want to smile but you have to sigh;
when care is pressing you down a bit,
rest, if you must, but don't you quit.
Life is queer with its twists and turns,
as every one of us sometimes learns,
and many a failure turns about
when he might have won had he stuck it out,
Don't give up though the pace seems slow.
You may succeed with another blow.
Success is failure turned inside out,
the silver tint of the cloud of doubt,
and you never can tell how close you are,
it may be near when it seems so far.
So stick to the fight when you're hardest hit.
It's when things seem worst you must not quit.

How appropriate. It surprised me how I was able to absorb the gist of the poem considering my mind kept wandering to John in the cubicle, willing him to get well. I took courage from the words, especially the final line which seemed to speak loud and clear. Things were at their worst and it was hard not to quit. But I drew determination not to lose hope, and trusted John would be alright. Eventually the Sister came into the office with the good news that John was now under control. I was so relieved! Dave arrived and together we sat by John's bedside grateful to see him fast asleep. The emergency was over.

Rev Kate Ricketts, the Hospital Chaplain, arrived soon after and we introduced ourselves. I was still a bit uptight at this point so I really appreciated her taking time to pray about the situation. She was keen to hear all about John, and the problems we'd had with him. She realised that with Dave training for the ministry she had a lot in common with us. We were to see a lot of Kate over the following months.

Due to the nature of this ward, each child was segregated into cubicles which are well equipped for their individual needs. Each room had a TV and video and being on the ground floor had French windows which opened out into the hospital grounds, ideal in the summer.

One cold January night I was miles away in thought as John toddled around the room. Aware of an unusual silence and a sudden cool breeze, I looked up to see the curtains blowing gently and the door ajar. The bold John was pottering around outside, clad only in his pyjamas.

How he managed to open the door remains a mystery, but it was just as well that I wasn't engrossed in a TV programme or he could've been over the border and far away! Hardly, since the area was securely fenced off, but nevertheless anything could have happened. The press would have had a field day with the morning's headlines: 'Careless Mother's In-Patient Becomes an Out-Patient in the Bitter Cold!'

The first six months seemed to fly past at Queen's. Despite John's frequent admissions to hospital, we had managed to settle quite happily. Even David was asking less and less for his old house now.

John's pattern of four convulsions every few weeks had continued notwithstanding the introduction of anti-convulsants; however, the fits occurred only during sleep. They could last for a few minutes or when more prolonged for over half-an-hour, but fortunately were not violent in nature. We kept a supply of medication at home to use in an emergency, and when administered it was usually successful in bringing the fits under control. However, on numerous occasions it had no effect, and we found ourselves rushing John into casualty for emergency treatment and admission. Each fit and each admission brought much heartache, fear and pain and once the crisis was over, great relief, joy and gratitude to the staff.

Family adjusting

Although we managed to cope initially, before long it began to tell on us as a family, especially young David. To begin with, he had gone obediently with his sisters

31

to whoever was available to look after them. But as the admissions and time spent apart increased he began to protest at being passed from pillar to post.

On one particular occasion he cried when he heard us say that John once again would need to go to hospital; so we felt justified in taking him with us. He took the emergency treatment John received in casualty and the transfer to the ward in his stride and was absolutely no trouble to us or the hospital staff, much to our relief.

Eventually one of the hospital teachers noticed David playing by John's bedside one day. Her general impression was that he had become a little introverted due to all the upheaval and attention John was having. Other than the initial bout of homesickness, we hadn't picked it up at all. He had always been a quiet little boy who could busy himself quite happily on his own; but now that it had been brought to our attention, perhaps she had a point.

The staff certainly welcomed siblings and encouraged them to visit, but it is not a normal environment for them and no matter how hard we tried they tended to get pushed a little to the side. The girls being at school spent less time on the ward than David, but on reflection, for him, it must have seemed a very long day.

The teacher suggested bringing David to the Hospital School where he could join in the many organised activities. We shall always be grateful to the teaching staff for the care and understanding they showed, and for all the work they did with David. He loved it. We travelled in from home together and before going over to the school, David would pop in to spend a little time with John. It was an ideal arrangement. He knew we were on hand if he wanted us but we never ever received an emergency call from the staff as he settled in very well to the routine. It made him feel like a *big boy* and he loved to tell his friends at the college that he'd been to school.

From that point onwards I always made an extra effort to talk to brothers and sisters of sick children who came to visit and made sure that they were included in conversations. They needed to know they were as important as the others and equally loved.

The girls were pleased to visit John in hospital when convenient, but were content to be cared for by friends when necessary. It eased our burden knowing they were not fretting, although on reflection I wonder if I didn't perhaps take them a little for granted at times. I always made an effort, though, to be with them on special occasions, so quite often I would find myself dashing home to curl hair for a party, or to attend a school function. Life had to go on.

At other times it was just to be with the children and to simply answer the run of the mill questions they bombarded me with; such as, 'Does God have any teeth?!' and 'Mummy, why have all those wrinkles come on your face? Does it mean you're going to die?!' Our children, not realising they were rubbing salt into the wound, often tactlessly reminded me that youth was slipping away fast, but so far they had managed to keep my secret!

CHAPTER 3

OUT OF CONTROL
(11th March–2nd April 1992)

In March the pattern changed dramatically. Not only did John's fits increase in number, but for the first time he had one when awake. As I was putting on his shoes, to my horror he keeled over and started to convulse. When it was over he seemed very sleepy. So we placed him on the couch and left him resting until our GP arrived. We were frightened for we knew that something was seriously wrong.

The children too, although so young, had seemed to sense this and often would whisper little prayers for him. That morning, during breakfast, I realised that young David was missing from the kitchen table. I peeped into the living-room and saw him kneeling by John's side, tenderly stroking his head; the love he had for his brother, so evident. As I stood in the doorway he looked up at me with such an expression of compassion on his face. 'He's lovely,' he said. Although David seemed unable to express his shock and fear during a fit, in his own way he was feeling the pain of it too. He was obviously as relieved as his parents that the fit had subsided and John was, for the present, able to rest.

Our GP arranged John's admission to hospital and I was once again involved in the familiar routine of caring for my son on the ward. This time, however, it was a nervous, weeping, frightened mother who watched over her child. At times I felt that being a trained nurse left me in an awkward position. I didn't want to jump in straightaway and tell everyone of my past occupation, with the result that members of staff would often say, 'Why didn't you tell us you were a nurse and save us going over that in detail?' It was important to me that my capacity as a mother came over more prominently than my nurse's training.

The rapport I had with the nursing staff could not have been better; they were wonderful and we got on so well together. Still I desperately missed close family and friends and felt I needed a shoulder to cry on. It's not the sick child who is looking for visitors but the child's parents, so when some of Dave's colleagues arrived from college, I was more than grateful to see them.

The most gorgeous display of flowers in a basket was delivered to our flat from the community at Queen's; they will never know what those flowers did for us. Many offered practical help; seeing the girls to school, or taking care of our household needs like shopping and ironing. Often we would return to find home-made cakes and scones at our front door. They shared how helpless they felt and made us promise that we would not hesitate to ask them for anything we needed, which was wonderful to know.

For the first few days John was averaging ten convulsions a day despite an increase in medication. Before long, however, the situation went completely out of control, resulting in a total of between thirty to forty.

When the consultant returned after the weekend, his words to me were, 'Mrs Hall, I am extremely worried about John.' To be worried myself was understandable, but when the consultant expressed his fears it had a paralysing effect on my whole being. Immediately he set the ball rolling and ordered as many tests as he could think of that would be relevant to John's situation. These included a CT Scan, an EEG, and numerous blood tests, all of which were reported as normal. Various anti-convulsants were introduced in high concentrations to try and control John's seizures but they had very little effect.

Eventually, he was showing signs of extreme heavy sedation which tore at our hearts and minds. He was unable to sit up, speak coherently, focus his eyes or hold his head still. Because his movements were so erratic, padding had to be placed around his cot to prevent him injuring himself. On one particular evening when Dr Rylance unexpectedly came into the ward, I burst into tears as I shared with him my fear that John must be suffering from some kind of brain damage. He reassured me by explaining that John's present behaviour was drug orientated and as soon as the levels of anti-convulsants settled in his system he would return to normal. What a relief to have that explanation!

We were heartened on the following day when Dave by John's bedside heard the little voice, that had been silent for days, saying, 'Harold.' Dave realised that the monitor at John's bedside was making a whirling noise, resembling the sound of the propellers of Harold the Helicopter from the 'Thomas the Tank Engine' Series.

As he was obviously responding to some external stimuli we were cheered up no end. For several days we continued to sing his favourite nursery rhymes and tell him familiar stories to see if this would stimulate him. However he seemed content just to listen and made no effort to communicate. Then on one occasion he responded as I repeated, 'The Fat Controller says, "You're a very naughty engine, Thomas"', from a Thomas the Tank Engine story. This had always made him laugh in the past, so when a smile appeared on his little face I could've kissed everyone in sight! It was a smile that shall always live in my memory.

Yet the trauma of the past few days began to tell. I had gone home for a few hours to see the other children and hopefully get some rest. (Dave's mother had come from Newcastle to lend a hand and what a stabilising force she was. We no longer had to find babysitters for the children which was one less problem to worry about.) But at home I couldn't settle, and became very anxious and low, being desperate to get back to John's bedside. A friend took me to the hospital and as I was leaving the car she put her arms round me and assured me of her prayers. Tears stung my eyes as I sobbed, 'What are we going to do?' I could sense her helplessness.

As I walked along the corridor, the thought suddenly struck me that, as a Christian, I must surely have something more in reserve than those who have no faith in God. So far all I seemed to have done since John's admission to hospital was cry. The nurses constantly brought me hankies and cups of tea. I had to get a grip of the situation.

Psalm 121 - A Spiritual Experience

It was early evening when I reached the ward. As John was fast asleep, I tiptoed round his cot and sat quietly beside him, my eyes still red from crying. It was then I read the words on a postcard pinned to the head of the cot. The card, which had been sent to John by one of Dave's colleagues from college, read *I will not let your footslip* (Psalm 121:3). I picked up my Bible and quietly read through the whole Psalm. What followed was undoubtedly the work of the Holy Spirit and could only be described as a 'quiet fire'. I was given power and peace and joy and strength in the midst of sadness; I discovered assurance and hope and the ability to praise God through pain.

Normally the ward was noisy, as all children's wards tend to be. One little lad used to ride his drip stand like a scooter from the top of the ward to the bottom; the racket caused by the over-burdened wheels bearing the weight of a ten year old was deafening. In addition, portable televisions blared out programmes from all four channels simultaneously. Yet on that Friday evening there was an unusual kind of quiet - a hush which permeated the four-bedded area where John slept. Nurses passed up and down, doctors, children and visitors too, but no one spoke to us, or said the customary 'hello' in the passing. It was almost as if John and I were invisible. I sensed a ring of peace and love surrounding John's cot as he slept. It was almost as if time stood still and no-one dared break the silence.

As I sat reading the psalm over and over again, I prayed and 'bathed' in the presence of the Holy Spirit.

God continued to speak to me clearly with words of assurance for John. I received so much that I thought I would burst with the joy that welled up in my heart. John slept through the whole experience, so as each new revelation arrived, I would slip my hand through the bars of the cot and rest them gently on him, praying the way I was being guided to by the Lord Jesus Christ.

I lift up my eyes to the hills - where does my help come from? My help comes from the Lord, the Maker of heaven and earth. I was conscious of looking upwards and asking the Lord for the help that we needed at that time. I knew from that moment He would give it to us. I believed in the Maker of heaven and earth, and at that moment was experiencing His presence in a most special way.

He will not let your foot slip. I looked at little John's feet as he slept, stroked them gently with my hands and whispered, 'John, Jesus will not let your feet slip, that's a promise.' I felt him safe in the Lord's care.

He who watches over you will not slumber; indeed, he who watches over Israel will neither slumber nor sleep. This spoke volumes to me as I realised for the first time in this situation that our Lord Jesus doesn't sleep! Like many mothers on the ward I slept on a mattress on the floor by my child's bedside. Due to the nature of John's illness I was afraid to fall asleep in case I failed to hear him in a fit, for if the nurses were busy at the other end of the ward they would miss it too. So I often lay awake listening out for John. Here, however, was the Lord telling me that He doesn't slumber nor does He sleep - He is available 24 hours a day. He would take care of John during the night. What a relief, with the sense of a burden lifted! I could feel the comfort flowing within as I repeated this verse to John several times.

The Lord watches over you - the Lord is your shade at your right hand; the sun will not harm you by day, nor the moon by night. When it dawned how much the Lord loved John and cared about him; that He was watching over him and would not let him come to any harm; nothing could hurt him, neither fits or drugs during the day or by night, I felt so elated. Again I prayed this verse over John and claimed the promise for him. 'John, the Lord is watching over you, darling, He won't let you come to any harm, sweetheart. He won't allow anything to hurt you at any time.'

The Lord will keep you from all harm - he will watch over your life; the Lord will watch over your coming and going both now and for evermore. Again the love and security came over in this verse. Yet what struck me most was the idea of *now*. The Lord was doing it *now*, not even sometime in the near future - but *now*. As John lay there I felt sure that he must be responding in some way to the peace and love present.

After I read the final verse to him I started at the beginning again and read through it in a whisper until I'd finally memorised it. I thought of the amount of times I'd read that psalm before, and yet never once did it have that kind of impact. How could a psalm written hundreds of years before be so contemporary? It was transforming my fears for John into something positive and sure. David the psalmist's needs were entirely different from John's and yet the words he used were so appropriate for us.

Although I didn't want the whole experience to end, I felt I had to share it with Dave's mother. Because I had left the house rather depressed and unhappy, I was convinced that this had 'rubbed off' on her. She was both delighted and relieved to hear how positive I was now feeling about John, and by the time the conversation was over she appeared much happier and grateful for fresh hope. It was a much calmer mother who settled down on the floor by her son's bed that evening; one who slept soundly because of a new found strength and confidence; one who was able to leave her little boy totally in the Lord's arms.

Baptism

For some time previously, I had felt strongly that the Lord was guiding us to have John baptised. I had said nothing to anyone, not even to Dave, as I wanted to have my feeling confirmed. We had considered the topic of baptism when our first child was born, but had prayerfully opted to have our children blessed and dedicated, leaving them with the freedom to accept or reject faith in the Lord Jesus. So here I was faced with an issue that more or less went against the grain. I prayed, 'Lord, if You want this for John, then please give me two confirmations?' The following morning I picked up a newspaper (which I very rarely do) and read an article about a little baby who had made a remarkable recovery from a serious illness following baptism. Confirmation No. 1!

Confirmation No. 2! came in an unusual way. I had popped home from the hospital to see the children.

Dave's mother told me a friend had just been on the phone and mentioned something about John being baptised. It meant very little to her but I was absolutely elated as I dialled the number to return the call. I discovered that the message was a little distorted. What had actually happened was that my friend had been praying for John and felt that at his baptism something had gone amiss which we ought to be praying specifically about. I decided to put her in the picture. Because I hadn't mentioned the question of baptism to anyone before, I felt that this very misunderstanding about it was my second confirmation.

However, a third came from friends at college, Kelvin and Catherine, not long after! When the issue of baptism arose during a conversation with them, they shared how strongly they had felt for some time that we should have John baptised, although up until this point they had never actually mentioned it to us.

Dave's tutor, the Rev Dr David Parker, was delighted to accept the invitation to baptise John. On March 21st 1992 he performed that beautiful sacrament. It was Saturday evening and once again the ward, dimly lit, seemed to have an air of tranquillity about it. Most of the children were asleep as David prepared John's bedside table. Dave, his mother and I gathered near to John, our eyes drawn to focus on the candle burning next to the cross. David spoke about baptism and read once more the psalm I had been so blessed with the previous evening. We prayed the Lord's Prayer together. I wondered what John made of it all, especially when the water was poured over his head, but his main concern was in blowing out the candle! - a sign for us that he was slowly returning to normal. It was a very moving service. Perhaps it was the venue, or simply because, 'where two or three are gathered ...'. I don't know, but it was a precious time; it was intimate; it was unique - almost crude - no baptismal gown, just a little lad in his pyjamas, a part of the sickness and suffering evident on the ward, who didn't understand the words, 'John, I baptise you in the name of the Father, the Son and the Holy Spirit.'

Getting John Under Control
It had been previously explained to us that the plan of action for John would be to try all available anti-convulsants in various doses and combinations. If this failed, a drug called Heminevrin given intravenously via a drip was often successful in controlling seizures, although it was not without risk. It would have to be commenced under the supervision of the ICU staff for it had been known in the past to cause respiratory depression. Finally, if this was unsuccessful then anaesthetisation would be the last resort.

This entailed using a drug called thiopentone to paralyse all the muscles, including respiratory, for a couple of days, making the use of a ventilator necessary. Of course all anaesthetics carry a risk, but in John's case it would be heightened due to the length of time he would be anaesthetised. This form of treatment was usually successful in breaking the fit pattern; so we trusted that in John's case it would have the desired effect should it become necessary to use it.

Over the weekend John improved slightly but by Monday morning his fits were once more on the increase and it became obvious that a change of treatment would be necessary. The consultant paediatrician covering for Dr Rylance, Dr De Belle, decided to take the bull by the horns and have John admitted to ICU for a Heminevrin infusion. As we wheeled him through the doors of Intensive Care I became very tearful. It seemed to me that we had been getting nowhere and were indeed going 'backwards'. I remember wanting to scream, 'He should be going out through the front doors of the hospital and home.' However, once he was settled and the infusion started I relaxed a little, hoping that th s would have the desired effect. It was explained to us that once the drug had reached a therapeutic level in John's system it would probably make him extremely drowsy and we were advised to go home for some rest. This we did once he was asleep, and were able to rest easy knowing he was in good hands.

The next morning the nurse looking after John shared with us, as she ducked to avoid a paper aeroplane he'd just fired, that he'd hardly slept a wink, and was full of beans. His hands were covered in red ink from the felt tipped pens he'd been scribbling with! We were amused to find him getting up to so much mischief, as we'd visualised him flat out all night. The nurse said it had been the best shift she'd had in ages, as the children they look after on the department are usually unconscious. That afternoon he was transferred back to Ward 6, but to our utter disappointment, the fits continued.

Early the following morning I realised John was

getting very little break between each fit, making the recording of them extremely difficult. By the time one fit was charted he was going into another one. The Ward Sister bleeped the registrar on call to put him in the picture and although he arrived on the ward soon after, it seemed to me we'd waited a life time. I've often seen actresses wringing their hands to emphasise their anxiety but can honestly never remember feeling the necessity to do likewise. However that Wednesday morning, before the doctor arrived on the ward, I stood doing just that whilst pacing up and down in sheer terror.

The Heminevrin infusion had been increased gradually over the past two days but it was having no effect. When Dr Barret arrived on the ward and suggested raising the dose again I burst out, 'Please, it's not doing any good, give him some diazepam.' He thought for a second as he looked from John to me, then asked for the drug keys, much to my relief. After just a couple of milligrams of the drug John settled and the fits subsided.

By this time I was in tears and felt physically drained. The Ward Sister phoned Dave to come straightaway, but he was leading a service in the college chapel at that time. His mother raced over to the chapel instead and had to interrupt the service to deliver the message. The staff and students were more than sympathetic and stood in for Dave, to allow him to be by my side. It was good to have him to share the burden, although I wished I could've coped more on my own. Dave was trying to hold his studies together as well as struggling through the nightmare with John.

We were praying desperately that John would not

need to be admitted to intensive care to be anaesthetised, so what joy as the day came and went and John remained fit free. By late evening his drip had to be removed, during which time he politely pulled out his naso-gastric tube! What a contrast to earlier in the day when he had looked so pathetic attached to so many tubes, leads and machines. He had perked up now and was back to being the John we were all so familiar with.

Several attempts were made to re-site the drip unsuccessfully so the mission had to be abandoned and his drugs given orally, much to John's relief. He could be heard all over the ward at 1.30 a.m. singing, 'Postman Pat,' calling, 'Hello Doctor,' and shouting for 'meat!' (John loved his food and always had a healthy appetite!) Dr Mitchell and the nursing staff were amused at this little performance and were as thrilled as we were that John's fits once again had been brought under control.

John remained unsteady on his feet but quite perky over the following few days. We spent as much of the day and evening with him either together, or if Dave had lectures, I would stay on my own. The only time John was ever left alone was when we went for a cup of tea or for some rest. He was quite happy with this arrangement and didn't seem to mind being left, although on the odd occasion he would cry crocodile tears which would dry up as soon as we were out of sight.

During one such absence, a student from Queen's popped into the ward to visit John. When he asked to see him, the nurse on charge questioned him about his identity. 'Can you tell me who you are?' (Quite rightly so, he could've been a total stranger.) Peter was taken aback and had a mental block as he struggled to sort out his relationship to John. Then he simply said, 'I'm his friend.' It seemed strange in a way for John to have such a 'grown up' friend, since we imagine children's friends to be around their own age.

Peter sat by John's bedside as he lay fast asleep throughout the visit. John adored Peter and would have loved it if he'd known he had come to see him. He often called his name at college and Peter would make such a fuss of him. When we returned to the ward and found the little car on John's locker we wondered who had left it. As Peter related the story later, I felt such a warmth and treasured what he had to share, especially his encounter with the nurse when he said, 'I'm his friend.' The words had such a soothing sound to them. What a fortunate little boy John was to have such a friend as Peter.

Dave decided that we all needed a holiday break to consolidate us once again as a family. Our other children were beginning to miss having John at home and the normal family routine, so we asked our consultant if it would be wise to take John on holiday once he was discharged. Fortunately he could find no reason why we shouldn't, but insisted that we take out insurance cover. I remember chuckling to myself at this as I reflected on a trip I'd made to India when I was single. I had no insurance cover at all (neither medical or for loss of personal belongings) and didn't even have a key to lock my suitcase. Completely nonchalant I was not surprised in the least, when at Delhi Airport my bulging white case appeared faithfully at 'baggage reclaim' intact and of course unlocked! But we carried out doctor's orders and got fully insured, fortunately.

Dave managed to get a last minute booking for a nostalgic trip to Jersey (where we had first met), much to the children's delight at the prospect of flying. I had trained in Jersey's General Hospital and knew that John would be well cared for should he require medical treatment during the holiday. However, an uneasy feeling lingered, which I found difficult to shake off.

John was discharged on 2nd April.

CHAPTER 4

INTENSIVE CARE AGAIN
(11th April-16th May 1992)

As the trip to Jersey approached, the children became more and more excited. I was very uneasy, however, about the holiday for I was of the opinion that it had been booked a little prematurely. Yet I decided to suppress my fears and show some enthusiasm by getting things organised. So for the first time in our family life, the cases were packed and ready a week before our expected date of departure; a feat, believe me! It would be wonderful if it all materialised; I dreamed. But it wasn't long before our holiday hopes were dashed.

A few days before we were due to set off, John was in severe trouble once again. By the time we reached the casualty department (on 15th April), he'd had at least 30 fits, the total reaching roughly 150 by the end of the afternoon. The amazing thing was, on the ward he stopped having fits at lunchtime, sat up, ate a two course meal, sang a few songs and became quite sociable before the fits resumed an hour later.

The Senior House Officer looking after John was most supportive and kept us informed of the plan of action to be taken. She was quite tearful when she broke the news to us that he would need to be admitted to ICU for anaesthetisation - it was the only hope of controlling him. Before he was transferred from the ward, she threw her arms around me and said, 'You must have nerves of steel.' We didn't. We felt a mixture of numbness, relief and apprehension. Numbness, due to the dreamlike daze we found ourselves in; relief, that soon John would be fast asleep on a ventilator, released from the exhaustion the fits were producing; and apprehension, as we were fully aware of the risks involved in this procedure.

We wheeled John into the bay prepared for him in ICU and were then shown to the parents' waiting room until he was safely on the ventilator. Dave and I sat next to each other wondering, 'Had it really come to this?' We chatted quietly until interrupted by Dr Rylance and the male nurse who had been designated to look after John. I can laugh now, but at the time I thought my world had ended. Dr Rylance entered the room looking rather serious and worried, although we didn't expect him to come in doing a song and dance! He explained to us that he would need a witness for what he was about to tell us, and introduced the male nurse.

The first thing that entered my mind was that there had been a complication during the intubation and John had arrested and died. I could feel the colour drain from my face with sheer anxiety, which Dr Rylance picked up immediately. He asked me if I was feeling alright and commented on my pallor! All I was capable of asking was if John was well. He assured us he was fine and continued explaining his intentions for John. By the time the interview was over my cheeks had returned to a healthier shade of pink, safe in the knowledge that John was still alive! I was afraid to share the real reason for my little 'turn' with Dr Rylance in case he thought me over-dramatic!

It was wonderful to watch John peacefully sleeping, even though it looked daunting seeing him 'wired up' to all those machines. The words that constantly entered my mind were, 'Bless him.' He was so unaware of all the heartache he was causing. The staff were marvellous and encouraged us to help with his care - swabbing his eyes and cleaning his mouth and so on. This helped to make us feel a little useful and pass the time, although there was always plenty of coming and going, and never a dull moment on this busy department. It amazed me how many staff were necessary for Intensive Care to function effectively, as we seemed constantly to see new faces.

Old memories resurface

They say in life you're kicked when down but one such 'new face', a young anaesthetist, had no idea the amount of upset he caused me each time he attended John. My first fiance had been killed in a road traffic accident many years before; the pain of that traumatic time goes without saying, but like many in similar situations I was able to pick up the pieces and find fresh meaning to life.

What a shock when I first saw this young doctor's face. Although not quite as tall, his face and colouring looked almost identical to that of my fiance. After the initial shock, I felt in a strange kind of way drawn to him and found it difficult to take my eyes off him. Hopefully he didn't notice this attraction and wasn't aware of the emotions I was struggling to stifle. But what guilt ensued! Why was I hoping to get another glimpse of this doctor? This was crazy, the past was gone and couldn't be brought back - this young man was not my fiance.

Basically these feelings had served to highlight the truth, that although I had been healed of the rawness and pain of my fiance's death and was a happily married mother, a scar had obviously remained and could easily open, but only if I was prepared to let it. It was not the time to mention it to Dave; he was going through enough already, but the memories stirring up inside caused such agony I wished I had someone to confide in. Here, brought together before my eyes, were the two most painful experiences of my life: one present, one a reminder of the past; and there in the midst of it all I desperately needed to find God.

We stayed by John's bedside until early evening; but soon the day's events began to catch up, leaving us both physically and emotionally drained. It had been a very full day. We were able to go home and take much needed rest, secure in the knowledge that John was being well cared for.

John's second birthday

The following day, 16th April, 1992, was John's second birthday. A beautiful birthday cake in the shape of one of his favourite characters, Fireman Sam and his engine, was made for him by Kelvin, a colleague of Dave's who had been a caterer before answering the call to the ordained ministry. It was absolutely tremendous and showed touches from the hands of a professional - almost too perfect to cut. John, for obvious reasons, couldn't have a birthday party and enjoy the usual celebrations, but nevertheless the day did have a special feel to it.

Although we didn't mention to any of the hospital staff that John was two that day, it was picked up by one of the doctors when she was writing his date of birth on a form. Before we knew it, the nurse looking after John had phoned the Play Therapist who arrived armed with balloons, and posters bearing the words, HAPPY 2ND BIRTHDAY JOHN.

She pinned all his cards on the wall including one with 'Thomas the Tank Engine' pictured on front which I knew he'd adore as soon as he was able to see it. If only he *was* awake to enjoy it. We took a couple of photographs but to be honest I felt rather silly attempting to keep things as normal as possible. How can you celebrate a child's birthday when he is unconscious? You have to ask yourself who's benefit you are doing it for, because it certainly isn't for the child's. I thought it better to have a birthday celebration once John was conscious and well enough to appreciate it - that made more sense to me.

Although Caroline, Louise and David were keen to visit their brother and bring their respective birthday presents, we postponed their visit, preferring them to see John awake rather than on a ventilator. However, the following day he was still unconscious and taking longer to rouse than anticipated, due to heavy sedation. I mentioned the wishes of our children to the consultant and shared my fears that seeing John in his present state might upset them. But he was of the opinion that there were some things in life children should be protected from, and this wasn't one of them. Therefore, he encouraged us to let them see John, providing we prepared them beforehand as to what to expect.

Initially they appeared a little wary but from there on they seemed to take the whole situation in their stride. They were quite happy to give John birthday kisses and certainly had no inhibitions as they sang, 'Happy Birthday'. We felt satisfied that we had allowed our children to visit John for it removed any mystery and fear they may have had about him.

My parents, however, who had come once again to help, found the experience less easy to handle, especially my mother who was extremely upset at seeing her youngest grandchild lying so helpless in a maze of tubes and leads. Whatever my father was feeling he kept to himself as he sat quietly gazing at John. They were due to return to Scotland that day, and offered to take our other children with them to compensate for the holiday they had lost out on. We agreed to this and Dave saw them safely to the station.

By early evening John eventually started to surface. It was wonderful to hear his little voice say, 'Bwoon' when he caught sight of the balloons suspended from the ceiling and 'Tank Engine' when he focused on the birthday cards. It was, of course, a joy to know he still recognised us and had come safely through the anaesthetic apparently none the worse. That same evening he was transferred back to Ward 6 and settled back to familiar surroundings.

Contact with other parents

A mother whose son was in the next bed to John got chatting with us and was interested to hear all about him. I shared briefly with her John's medical problems to date, but by the time she had related her son's heart-breaking story to us, we felt like screaming - not because we were hard or insensitive, but because over a period of time, the pain of being involved with sick children starts to have an effect on you. My heart went out to them, and they felt for us, but some days were more intolerable than others and this, for us, was one of those days. Intensive Care was such an eye-opener, and had taken its toll with us emotionally over the past few days.

The quick turnover of patients on the ward didn't help much either. Some children were only in hospital for a day or two, so I found myself repeating 'John's story' to their parents over and over again when each new admission arrived. Often it helped to be thick-skinned as well! One woman said during our conversation, 'Your son's got a big head, hasn't he?' First I'd heard of it, but preferred not to agree with it! (Later John's head circumference proved to be, in actual fact, *smaller* than the family average. Not unless we're a family of big heads!)

Some parents were genuinely interested whilst others were simply nosey. I'll never forget one day on the ward when John was in a full-blown grand mal fit. One mother was sitting on the window ledge in the ward with her child, and actually moved closer to John's cot to get a better view of him convulsing! Others were so full of love and concern for John as we were for their children, that the support we gave each other was invaluable and a saving force on many a day.

The day after John was discharged from Intensive Care he seemed much improved. By early evening, however, when we were bathing him we noticed some neck stiffness and an inability to bend his head forward. Frights like these often plagued us and served to add to the frustration and worry we were already experiencing with him. My first impression was that he was suffering from meningitis so I immediately called for the Sister in charge. She reassured us and advised us to go home for a rest once we'd settled him down. Although we were reluctant to go, we were so exhausted that we were forced to take her advice.

She told us later that she had not wanted to alarm us needlessly since we had just been through so much. However, as soon as we had left the ward she had phoned the doctor on call, fearing that John had contracted meningitis. Whatever the cause we never found out, but by the following morning he was a little better and the neck rigidity gone. Yet another little emergency over.

Easter Time

It was Easter Sunday. Dave and I had the opportunity to attend the service in the hospital chapel and although numbers were few, we found what was shared very moving. A couple of days before on Good Friday, we had been thinking of Christ's death on the cross and the pain and suffering He endured to save mankind from sin. Now two days later we were celebrating the victory; His resurrection. The day when He rose again. By dying on the cross and rising again, a pathway to eternal life was established for those who would love Him and put their trust in Him. As I thought about the meaning of Easter in relation to what had been happening to John over the past few days, it occurred to me that we'd had, in a way, our own little resurrection to thank God for; the connotation being kind of special.

Back on the ward, various charities had been round the ward delivering Easter eggs to the children. Members from the hospital radio station, 'Radio Lollipop', had arranged for the pop group 'UB40' to visit that same afternoon. They arrived on the ward with their entourage close behind, armed with hats, T-shirts, stickers and badges.

However, they appeared to make more of an impression on the parents than the children! In fact, the children really didn't have a clue as to who they were, especially John, but I asked if he could have his picture taken with them anyway. He was given a hat bearing the group's name and allowed to keep it after the photo, much to Dave's delight! The following morning it was the parents who were sporting 'UB40' T-shirts and not the children for whom they were intended!

By Easter Monday John had made such a remarkable recovery that the nurse looking after him called to me as I entered the ward, 'There's a new wee boy here, I don't know if you'll recognise him.' It was such a relief and pleasure to see him looking so bright and cheerful and calling to us as soon as he saw us. He was singing and running around the ward full of mischief and so full of life. The change in him was wonderful to see and caused a happiness to well up that made me whisper inside, 'Lord, thank You once again for getting us through another traumatic time.'

A special MRI Scan was arranged for the following month at the Nuffield Hospital which was conveniently 'over the hedge' from the college. This scan shows in much more detail sections of the anatomy, and was therefore more accurate than the previous CT scans John had had in the past.

The possibility of a tumour had been mentioned as a root cause of these multiple convulsions. Had this been suggested many months before, we would have been struck with terror at the thought of it, but this was no longer the case. We had come to the point of actually hoping something would show up; something to account for the number of fits he was having; something that would give us a diagnosis; something that would respond to treatment and enable us to put the nightmare well behind us. Such was our desperation.

When your child is ill you want everything possible done for him immediately, so over a period of many months we learned the true meaning of patience as we'd never learned it before. We had to wait for appointments, for tests and then for results. The fact that there were other sick children to be cared for as well as John, protected us from selfishness.

John was discharged a couple of days later and his regime of anti-convulsants explained to us. We decided to travel up to Scotland straightaway whilst the going was good, as we had come to realise that there was no definite pattern now and John could start fitting at any time.

The journey, by car, that afternoon was extraordinary to say the least. Granted, the conditions were perfect for travelling, but we were both aware of a feeling of being protected as we journeyed. There was actually a sensation at times, almost as if the car was flying (that was without breaking the speed limit!). We both believe the car was surrounded by angels guarding our path and nothing could convince us otherwise. Neither of us has experienced anything like it before, but would welcome a similar journey any time, especially during traffic jams!

It was lovely to see our children again, our family and friends, and just to have John so well. On the way back south we stopped off at Newcastle to visit Dave's family for a few days. We took John to the church his parents attended and were delighted at the response of the congregation who'd been praying fervently for him. It was difficult to tell how ill John had been. He was racing around with the other children having a marvellous time; the only indication of any recent problem showed in his slight loss of balance. We travelled back to Birmingham that day as a family, once again with hope in our hearts that John's fits would soon cease.

The EEG the following day was reported normal. We were delighted as we had been told previously that John would never have a normal result again. However, our elation was soon brought abruptly to an end when the fits returned once more. Since being anaesthetised he'd had only twelve clear days, so it was becoming obvious that the time lapse between each period of fits was decreasing, whilst the number of convulsions was increasing - this is apparently a strange phenomenon observed by the medical profession.

By the time the appointment for the MRI Scan had come round, John was once again a patient in the Children's Hospital, so we could not conveniently 'jump over the hedge' into the Nuffield Hospital, but instead would now have to go through the normal channels. Pity!

It seemed that everything was hanging on this scan as every other relevant test had been carried out and John had been seen by both medical and neurological teams in the search for a diagnosis.

MRI Scan

The night before the scan, it took me longer than usual to fall asleep. I lay on the floor next to John's cot pondering over the following day's plans and arrangements. I felt a little anxious, but pleased at the prospect of knowing that by this time tomorrow we would no doubt be nearer to a diagnosis. Even if a full report wasn't available, at least we'd know if the scan was 'all clear' or showed 'something'. For some time my mind had been going round in circles wondering what could possibly be causing this illness.

The MMR injection was often top of the list; after all John had been perfectly healthy up until he was immunised and it seemed too much of a coincidence when he fitted only a few days later - but to cause so many fits? Then I'd blame the tetanus injection I'd had during pregnancy, convincing myself that in some way it must have been responsible for causing his brain to develop abnormally in the womb. At one point I believed John was fitting in response to some internal pain and kept pleading with the doctors to consider this possibility, after all they were as baffled as we were and could offer no full explanation. Finally I convinced myself John must have some food allergy since he often fitted shortly after eating or drinking. For months I continued to observe, diagnose and basically nearly drive myself crazy, but tomorrow we'd know!

When John awoke I bathed and dressed him so that he would be prepared in plenty of time for the arrival of the ambulance. It seemed that the whole ward knew where we were going, as on leaving with a nurse escort, we received plenty of well wishes from Ward staff and patients' relatives. Dave met us at the Nuffield Hospital, only to be told by the receptionist that there was a technical problem with the scanner and it would take an hour before they would know if it would be functional that day or not. We decided to pop over to our flat for a coffee to kill time and let John play with his own toys for a little while. The receptionist agreed to phone us as soon as she had any information; this she did an hour later, explaining that the scanner would be in operation in a couple of days' time. A return appointment was made for then and we returned to the ward rather disappointed at the morning's outcome. All I could think of was how I was going to stay patient for a further two days until John had the scan.

The next day Dave's mother was arriving from Newcastle to help once again. It seemed to take our minds off the scan for a little while, so before we knew it, Wednesday afternoon had arrived, and so had the ambulance for John.

On arrival at the Nuffield Hospital, the first question the Radiologist asked was if John had been sedated. He was rather annoyed to discover he hadn't, but decided to give him some diazepam intravenously which would hopefully knock him out. As John lay on the table in the scanning room, wide-eyed, we used every trick in the book to get him to sleep but to no avail. We sang endless rounds of the 'Snowman', 'The Little Mermaid', 'The Spirit of the Lord', and any of his favourites that came to mind whilst we stroked his head and held his hand. Yet even with lights dimmed, it unfortunately had no effect.

The Radiologist gave him yet another dose of diazepam, bringing the total to 10 mgs, which would knock the average adult out, but not John. In fact, he seemed to have more life and was amazingly restless. Since it was imperative that he lie completely still throughout the whole procedure, it was decided to abandon the mission and an appointment was given for two days' time. What followed in reception could only be described as a complete and utter pantomime!

Dave was so frustrated at the afternoon's events that he could be heard complaining first to the radiologist, then to the nurse, then back to the radiologist and to whoever else happened to cross his path in between as he paced up and down the reception area. For a change(!) I was sitting bubbling at the thought of having to wait yet another couple of days before we would be any nearer to a diagnosis; I felt robbed of the tiny amount of patience

I had left. The receptionist brought me coffee in a huge breakfast cup that could've housed a few goldfish, and as I sat sniffing, wiping tears and slurping coffee, John was skelping around the reception area as high as a kite, shouting, 'Hello Doctor!' The nurse who had escorted us was on the phone to sort out transport to take us back to the ward and as I sat there amidst the commotion, completely stunned, all I could think of was, 'What a fiasco!'

The Ward Sister apologised to us for not sedating John before he left the ward, but she explained that she was unhappy to transfer a sedated child by ambulance to another hospital without a doctor escort. Tearfully, I accepted this and continued to chase John up and down the ward for the remainder of the day before he finally conked out at 10 pm! Dave's mother told me later that when she heard about the afternoon's events, she took her frustration out on our kitchen wall by scrubbing the stains off vigorously. (One consolation was the remarkable difference in the kitchen wall, it had never been so clean!)

Friday morning heralded the third attempt. John had slept all night and had remained fit free since the dose of diazepam he'd been given two days previously. It seemed a shame, but after I woke him up, bathed and dressed him, he was given sedation to 'knock him out' in preparation for the scan. It wasn't long after his little eyes closed over and he was fast asleep that the ambulance arrived and we set off with Dr Akbar, our escort, who had come to know John well. During the journey, Dr Akbar chatted about John, then pulled out of his notes an article from the *Lancet* which had been written by Dr Rylance entitled, *Treatments of Epilepsy and Febrile Convulsions in Children*. It seemed ironic he should have someone in his care like John who blew all his theories! Whoever placed the article in John's notes obviously did it with tongue in cheek!

On arrival at the Nuffield Hospital, I could hardly look the receptionist in the eye as I was convinced I could read her thoughts, 'Oh no, not the Hall's again!' However, we were welcomed and offered the customary cup of coffee whilst John was being transferred from the ambulance to the scanning room. Just as he was placed on the table his little head popped up and his voice, which sounded as rough as sandpaper with tiredness, informed us, 'Johnny's better now.' I thought, 'Oh no, he can't be waking up,' but fortunately, much to our great relief, he laid down immediately and slept soundly throughout the next hour.

We were watching the pictures of John's brain as they appeared on the screen and marvelling at modern technology. The scan was clear, which in one way we were pleased about, and yet deep down we wondered where that really left us. But John was allowed home that day and for the present we were just rejoicing at getting over yet another nightmare.

A prayer request book lay permanently on the table in the hospital chapel. It was well used by many from all walks of life and cultures. Some obviously had a strong faith in God, whilst others were trying to muster even the tiniest amount of belief. This was apparent by the content of their prayers which were so varied.

Before we took John home that day we entered our own prayer of thanksgiving and gratitude:

Lord, thank You once again for getting us through another nightmare with John. We pray that You will grant him health to enjoy Your beautiful sunshine. We pray in the name of Jesus Christ, our Lord and Master, Eleanor and Dave.

Our relief and rejoicing lasted only several hours before the fits returned and we were back to square one. We managed John at home over the weekend but it was heartbreaking watching him lying on a mat on our living-room floor getting very little break at all. It was the month of May and the weather was glorious. Outside, the children from college were running around enjoying the sunshine, but although we knew John should be playing with them, there was very little chance of him joining them.

A friend popped in to visit and was horrified to witness three fits in fifteen minutes. We had known John to have five fits in five minutes; it's surprising how accustomed you can get. In the early days, when John was taking four fits every six weeks, we were absolutely devastated - now we would've settled for four fits every day. At least we would've known where we stood. In this situation, we never knew how long each fit was going to last, or how many he would have before getting a break, and of course how long that break would be. We had often wondered how long it would take before he started to show some kind of deterioration as a result of them, and believed that the time had actually arrived, since he had started to lose weight.

He had always been such a happy little boy, full of life and energy, but recently we noticed he had become quite fractious and difficult to motivate. Since it was obvious the anti-convulsants were having very little, or no effect, and he couldn't spend every other week in ICU anaesthetised, we wondered what, if anything, was left to help him? Could we continue living the way we were doing this weekend, counting fits and having no proper family life? Watching our little son existing with such a poor quality of life was becoming unbearable.

We had often prayed to the Lord to heal John either divinely or through the hands of the medical profession, but so far that healing had not been granted. Was the Lord trying to show us something through this? If so, we certainly couldn't put our finger on it. We were grateful for our faith in Christ and felt Him very close to us, sustaining us, and hard as it may be to believe, we were able to praise Him through the pain and suffering.

CHAPTER 5

I'LL GIVE YOU BACK A HEALTHY CHILD
(17th May-30th May 1992)

It was during one of these 'praise times' one evening that I received a most wonderful promise from our Heavenly Father; a promise that was to sustain me when all hope seemed lost. Dave and I had gone to bed and were talking about John and where it was all leading. We eventually started singing to God and praising and thanking him even though we were heartbroken, and even though the situation remained unchanged. We just 'let go' and sang without any inhibitions, whatever hymn or worship chorus came to mind, feeling much better for the release it brought, however incredible that may sound.

We had prayed so often before for a diagnosis. The fact that our prayer had not been answered as yet, did not prevent us from persevering. Just before we were about to start praying for John that evening, I suggested to Dave that we might sit in silence and allow the Lord time to 'speak' to us. This we did, and shortly after we began, I heard clearly the words, *'I'll give you back a healthy child.'*

I knew instantly that these words were from the Lord. What I couldn't understand was where God was taking John first, before we were to have him back. I'll give you *back* a healthy child; that was in fact revealed to us much later. We had listened and the Lord had spoken and that was very comforting. We weren't given a diagnosis; instead God, in His wisdom, gave us a promise, a promise which rang true and clear over the following few weeks, and one which I was able to hang on to through the darkness.

When I shared with Dave what had just transpired, he didn't comment there and then, but much later he told me he had interpreted the words to mean we'd lose John and have another child in his place. But I had no doubt in my heart - this promise was for John!

On the Monday morning I was forced to contact Dr Rylance who agreed to see John in casualty. He could see clearly that John wasn't his normal self and could understand our concern. It was decided that the time had come to give steroids a try. We were reluctant, but again felt we had no option, and in a way were looking forward to the increase in appetite (a common side-effect of this drug) which we hoped would help to build John up and, of course, stop his fits. I honestly did not think it would, but I didn't voice my opinion. The following day John had to be re-admitted to Ward 6. He needed to be under constant medical supervision due to his deteriorating condition.

One of the relief consultants once said to us that if John presented in casualty having these multiple fits, they would be running around pulling all the stops out and carrying out emergency care. He felt the fact that John could have twenty fits, stop, sit up in bed and sing a round of the 'Snowman' before lying down again when the fits resumed, had perhaps caused them to become rather complacent.

Up until this point John had never injured himself during a fit. One afternoon, however, when Dave's mother and I were by his bedside on the ward, he had his thumb in his mouth when he took a fit. We were both in tears as we struggled to free his thumb from his clenched teeth, but to no avail. We could only wait helplessly until the fit subsided, leaving a cut so deep we could almost see the bone. The nurses dressed the wound to prevent infection and like us were diligent in making sure his fingers were kept out of his mouth in future.

By the Saturday we had decided to accept my parents' offer and take the children up to Scotland to spend their school holidays there. Dave dropped us off at the station where I purchased the tickets only a few minutes before the train arrived at the platform. Because of such a late booking we could not reserve seats, which made things a little difficult as the train was busy and any empty seats had 'reserved' tickets on them. We were forced to sit down on four such seats until the congestion in the passageway eased.

I felt absolutely exhausted, and also guilty at having to leave John in hospital. Tears were flowing down my cheeks when, to my surprise, the lady sitting behind tapped me on the shoulder and assured me; 'Don't worry dear, you'il get a seat.' You'll get a seat! I had to laugh. If that was my only worry I'd have been on cloud nine. As I turned to explain our situation I noticed that the 'reserved' tickets on the back of our chairs were out of date. What a relief to be able to officially sit there for the remainder of the journey.

I stayed with my parents for a couple of days, but by Monday morning I was desperate to get back down to Birmingham to see John as I was missing him so much. Caroline, Louise and David were quite content at their grandparents' home and happy to see old friends again, so I knew I could return to the hospital with an easy mind. Dave had informed me over the phone that there had been very little change. I arrived in the evening to find John fast asleep, and although desperate to hold him tightly in my arms, I decided to leave him sleeping as it was wonderful to see him so peaceful.

Dave and I had discussed the prospect of taking John up to Newcastle for a few days to visit Dave's parents and family before travelling on to Scotland to collect our children. Our reasoning was that really nothing more was being done for John in the ward that we couldn't do for him at home. We were charting all his fits and generally taking care of him anyway and, of course, would be able to continue his medication at home. The only worry was that if John got into some difficulty and needed medical help, would we be near enough to a children's hospital? We would certainly be able to give a clear history to any doctor should that be necessary, but obviously a cover letter would be of value in case of any emergency.

Dr Plant felt that our family needed a complete break without the responsibility of John, and suggested that we go up north and leave him in their care. He said, 'I know you won't go for a holiday without him, but that's what I honestly feel you need.' We appreciated his concern for us and could see the wisdom in his advice, but we couldn't do it - we just couldn't leave John.

During the ward round the following morning, we discussed our plans with the Registrar, Dr Williams, and were quite taken aback at how willing he was to allow John leave of absence. We both felt a strange feeling that for some reason we were doing the right thing, however risky that might be.

Dave's family was quite shocked at how thin John had become and how poorly he looked. They were also disturbed to see, for the first time, their little nephew convulsing. The weather was glorious during the few days we spent in Newcastle, but it could hardly be enjoyed to the full with John lying on a mattress in the garden for several hours at a time, getting very little break between fits. His appetite was so poor that if he managed a yoghurt or a banana, Dave's mother and I were delighted.

By the time we arrived in Scotland John had begun to deteriorate dramatically. We were aware that he had stopped speaking and was tending to stare through us rather than focus properly with his eyes. We wondered if the heavy dose of anti-convulsants together with the steroids were to blame. It was a strange experience to find your child unable to communicate as before. I wanted to shout, 'Answer me John, answer me', but I knew for the moment communication was impossible. By Saturday we were forced to take him into Yorkhill Children's Hospital in Glasgow as the situation had worsened. Not only had he stopped eating and talking, but his eyes were now fixed obliquely to his left. He was seen in Casualty before being admitted to Ward 5b.

CHAPTER 6

A DIAGNOSIS
(1st June-5th June 1992)

The following afternoon we were heartened to hear from the Senior Registrar examining John, that the consultant neurologist, Dr. Stephenson, was extremely interested in patients suffering from convulsions and he was expected back the next morning. Apparently he had written a book about *Fits, Faints and Funny Turns*. We found the alliteration in the subject matter quite amusing and wondered if in any way it reflected the character of the author. (It did!)

First thing on Monday morning Dr Stephenson arrived in our cubicle, introduced himself, and took a brief history of John's story to date. He wanted to see one of John's convulsions first hand, so we were asked to call him on the ward as soon as one developed. This we did, and were impressed firstly by the interest he showed in John and secondly by his skill as a neurologist. He was incredible. He watched every movement of John during the fit, then pointing to the left upper part of his forehead, announced, 'That's where his problem lies.'

Within half an hour Dr Stephenson had arranged a CT Scan. As he helped push John on the trolley (at a fair pace!) along the corridor to the scanning room, he was writing John's notes, and asking further pertinent questions. Everything seemed to be happening so quickly, but our prayer was that it would be a step towards finding a diagnosis. He felt sure that the CT Scan was not completely negative, so to back up his findings, he arranged for John to have a special SPECT Scan in a neighbouring hospital.

The remarkable thing was that there were only two of these scanners in the country - one in Glasgow and the other in London. If John had needed admission to hospital when we were visiting in Newcastle, that same facility would not have been available there to aid the diagnosis. We now believed the Lord had guided us to Glasgow at just the right time and were so grateful that He did.

Dr Stephenson also arranged for John, during his convulsions, to be videoed for several hours and for the MRI Scan pictures to be sent from The Children's Hospital in Birmingham. He altered John's medication but, unfortunately, this had very little effect in controlling the fits. We were pleased when he stopped the steroids since they had not had the desired effect; in fact we felt, rightly or wrongly, that they were in some way aggravating his condition.

The evening before the scan, as I sat quietly by John's bedside, I found myself pleading with the Lord to make the scan proceed without a hitch. Perhaps the memories of the MRI Scan he had in Birmingham were lingering, rather too fresh for comfort, in my mind! In the past, it had seemed that whatever we had prayed for regarding John had not been granted. We had prayed he

wouldn't need medication, but he did; we had prayed that
the number of fits wouldn't increase, but they did; we
had prayed that he wouldn't need to be anaesthetised, but
he was; and yet we were not put off by this apparent
failure in prayer; prayer was our lifeline. So, still
trusting God to answer, I desperately pleaded, 'Please
Lord, let everything work out tomorrow as planned.'
Many friends and family members were behind us,
which was a comfort in itself.

SPECT Scan

We were transferred to the Southern General Hospital
by minibus along with a nurse escort, who stayed with
us for the duration of the procedure. We were made
welcome on the day ward and John was safely placed in
a cot. To get the clearest picture and scan result, John
needed to fit during the injection of the radioactive
material, but would have to lie perfectly still for one hour
during the actual scan. The way John had been recently
made this seem like a tall order. The EEG technicians
arrived and started running off a trace during which John
had a couple of seizures. They immediately contacted
the radiographer who arrived a few minutes before
John's next fit and made ready the necessary injection.
This was given exactly on time leaving only one hurdle
to go. John's fits were running around every 20-30
minutes which made lying still for one hour during the
scan seem impossible.

He was transferred to the X-ray department by
trolley and on to the bed in the scanning room. This
upheaval had obviously not disturbed him, because he

lay fast asleep and fit free during the whole procedure! We could hardly credit it. Our prayers had indeed been answered - everything had gone according to plan. When Dr Stephenson saw the pictures, he commented on their quality and praised John for doing everything right. It was round about this time we started to feel that we'd reached a turning-point and that things were now starting to move, and for the very first time the 'brick wall', at long last, was losing height.

The scan confirmed Dr Stephenson's suspicions that John was suffering from a congenital disorder called Cortical Dysplasia. Since it was obvious he was not responding to medical treatment, and the number of fits were not decreasing, it was felt that John would be a good candidate for neurosurgery. Since we were living in Birmingham and neurosurgery was available at the Children's Hospital, it was decided that we should return there for the operation.

CHAPTER 7

BACK TO BIRMINGHAM
(6th June – 16th June 1992)

On Saturday, 6th June, we tackled the five hour journey by car from Glasgow to Birmingham, keeping a record of John's fits throughout the journey. The other children were marvellous and very sympathetic towards their little brother. Children seem to sense a situation and often rise to the occasion, so for that particular journey they could not have been better behaved. We were relieved to arrive safe and sound on Ward 6 and the welcome we received from staff and parents made it feel like we had come home. A cot had been made ready for John in his usual spot in the four-bedded bay, across from Natasha and Carrie Anne his friends, which we thought was such a lovely touch. We were getting to know the staff on the ward so well by this time and appreciated the help and support they gave us.

John continued to convulse over the weekend, so by Monday morning we were desperate to see the consultant, Dr Rylance, to find out how John was to be managed. We discovered during the ward round, much to our utter disappointment, that he would not be back till Wednesday morning, resulting in John being cared for by the Registrar. I shared with him my fears that if John was allowed to continue fitting without any further medical intervention until Wednesday, he would suffer some kind of damage to his brain. The Registrar and House Officers who examined John that day listened to my fears sympathetically, but what followed mid-morning took me as much by surprise as it did Dave and the nursing and medical staff.

John's convulsions had up until this time been fairly gentle, and latterly, quite short in duration. As I stood by his bedside during one particular fit I noticed that it was developing into quite a violent one. It had started in the usual manner, but when he reached the jerking stage (clonic stage) his wee head was actually banging off his pillow. All I remember thinking was, 'I can't stand this any longer, watching my son (what I could only describe as) being tormented.' I started sobbing uncontrollably and screaming, 'Someone has got to help him; stop his suffering. Will someone please help my wee boy?' Dave was holding me in his arms, trying to fight back his tears.

It was a very strange experience to hear this loud, wailing noise and realise I was the one responsible for it. It was certainly audible at the other end of the ward, because nurses and a doctor came running behind the screens that had been pulled by a parent to give us privacy. She knew John well and was obviously upset by what was happening. I actually felt I was about to 'crack' and could not hold back my anguish any longer. I pleaded with the House Officer as he administered an intravenous drug to John, 'Please do something; is there another consultant who could see John today?'

Dr Goldstein was that consultant. We warmed to her

immediately as she had such a caring and sympathetic bedside manner. It was easy to put our trust in her as we found her both competent and compassionate. She agreed that John was deteriorating and would need intensive care therapy that same day. We were so relieved to have him transferred to ICU and to see him sleeping peacefully on a ventilator, out of his misery. What was envisaged was John being kept on the thiopentone infusion for a couple of days as before, then gradually being weaned off the drug and ventilator. This, it was hoped, would give him a fit free period, long enough for the medical staff to make the necessary preparations for brain surgery, and to build John up, for he had very little stamina and had grown extremely thin.

We were given a room in the Parents' Block which was a God-send, as this allowed us to be on hand at all times. It was ideally situated above the chapel which was next to the Intensive Care Unit. The rooms were basic but adequate and always very quiet. Many parents sought solace there and we were no exception.

The following day Dave's mother arrived from Newcastle to look after our children, leaving us as much time as we needed to be with John. She visited John regularly and although she found it difficult seeing him so ill, she was a strength to us. There was always a sense of 'everything is going to be alright' when she sat by his bedside; love just radiated from her being. If this love alone could have healed John, the healing would have been instantaneous. Our other children visited John regularly, fortunately without getting too upset as they had grown accustomed to seeing him in ICU. When we took them for a drink from the machine, or to the outdoor play area, it was like an adventure to them.

Parents of children on Ward 6, with whom we had become friendly, were a great support to us and were able to take the latest news about John back to those in the ward who knew him. It was wonderful to know everyone was rooting for us. We were often stopped in the corridor or in the dining-hall by those keen to have an update on his condition; although it was constantly 'good news, bad news' - our hopes raised, only to be dashed again - but our love for John kept us going.

By Thursday, John required a blood transfusion and despite intensive physiotherapy to his chest developed pneumonia; so he was commenced on antibiotics. On top of this he wasn't absorbing his feeds through the naso-gastric tube which was his only source of nutrition - he could have done without this setback as he was already underweight. The thiopentone was discontinued, so I took a little comfort in the knowledge that he'd be 'round' in a couple of days and able to eat a normal diet soon after. Nevertheless the day's events left me feeling quite down. A little doubt had crept in - had the Lord really given me the words, 'I'll give you back a healthy child?' Before leaving for home that night, I popped into the hospital chapel and wrote the following prayer in the prayer book: *Father, I ask You to help my wee son John and confirm Your word to me. I pray in the precious name of Jesus Christ.*

When we arrived home, Dave's mother was laughing to herself as she related a conversation she'd had with Caroline. At bedtime they'd been saying prayers for

John when Caroline suddenly said, 'Grandma, John is going to be alright. I can hear a voice telling me, and it's coming from your stomach!' Dave's mother hid her grin and astonishment and continued praying, when to her amazement a few moments later, Caroline insisted once more, 'Grandma, I can hear that voice from your stomach again saying everything is going to be alright with John!' We were having a laugh at the episode and discussing the unusual things children say, when suddenly the prayer request I'd placed in the book sprung to mind. In this strange and most unexpected way, God had confirmed His words to me: I'll give you back a healthy child. Dave reminded us that the stomach (bowel) at one time was regarded as the seat of the emotions in Old Testament tradition, so perhaps Caroline hadn't been so far wrong after all ... and a little child shall lead them (Isaiah 11:6 RSV).

By the time Saturday arrived, John was showing signs of gaining consciousness, but unfortunately he was also showing signs of convulsing and had to be recommenced on thiopentone. We knew this was serious and it seemed that John wasn't going to get the chance of a couple of weeks respite before surgery.

We were introduced to Mr Walsh the neurosurgeon, who explained to us his intentions regarding John's surgery. He had originally planned to operate a week later but, due to John's deteriorating condition, had decided to bring the operation forward to Wednesday, 17th June, 1992, a date I shall never forget.

Glasgow had already been contacted to request a copy of the SPECT Scan pictures and reports which he would need before he could operate. Dave completed the consent form for the operation and Mr Walsh explained a little of what he planned to do. He would remove the part of the left frontal lobe of John's brain where the main focus of abnormal electrical activity appeared to be. But he felt it was too risky to be totally radical as he feared John would be left either paralysed down his right side or have a marked weakness there. If he could have done the complete operation he could have given us an 80-90% guarantee that John would remain fit free or at least be reduced to only one or two fits per year, but now the percentage lay at 50/50.

Mr Walsh also explained that although he would need John to have one or two fits during surgery to enable him to locate the area affected, ideally he would prefer him to be out of status pre-operatively, as no neurosurgeon would normally consider operating on a fitting brain. But it looked like he would have to do just that, as John was proving too difficult to control. The more we heard, the more we realised nothing was going well for our son - he really wasn't in the best operable state. But we felt we had no option but to allow surgical intervention; it was his only chance. One other problem which would need to be outruled during surgery was the possibility of a condition known as Encephalitis. Should this be present then the prognosis for John would be poor since surgery is of no value in this disease.

As we slowly soaked in what was transpiring, we realised that we would need to pray for strength to go through the next few days. The reality of the last few months seemed more like a dream that was slowly turning into a nightmare, and like all nightmares we had very little control over the outcome. At times we found it difficult to pray - even *how* to pray - but we still believed John was in God's hands. Dave and I often used the Hospital Chapel, which was conveniently next door to ICU, to meditate or to make use of the prayer request book. A few moments away made all the difference and seemed to strengthen us. On many occasions I simply sat down and played the piano there which I found therapeutic. When I was in a sober, pensive mood, I would play anything from Beethoven's 'Fur Elise,' to 'Cavatina', to that beautiful worship song, 'So Freely'; but when feeling angry or frustrated, I would bash out James Taylor's 'Fire and Rain' which was preferable to kicking the cat!

On Sunday morning Dave was preaching at a church near Bromsgrove and, although he could've cancelled the appointment, he felt strongly that he should carry on. Many were blessed by what he had to share and told him so after the service. His mother especially felt comforted and was glad she had gone along to hear her son preach.

One of the Sunday School teachers later told Dave that when she had announced in the class that it was time for prayers, before she got the chance to start, our daughter Louise suddenly began praying out loud, 'Dear Lord, please make my wee brother better.' The teacher was taken aback at the spontaneity of this little girl who was obviously sharing in the suffering of her family. Our children tended to carry on as usual and at times we never really knew what they were thinking about John, but here was proof that in their own unique way they were also feeling the pain.

I remember one day sitting with Dave at John's bedside, and looking around the unit at the other unconscious children and thinking, 'Not one of these little ones deserves to be here. If I go out into the street I won't find any child out there either who deserves to be in their place.' I tried to reason suffering out.

Sometimes we can bring sickness and suffering upon ourselves; drug abuse, in its various forms, being a prime example; or the young 'joy-rider' who smashes a car and ends up fighting for his life in hospital; or the person harbouring bitterness and resentment, two emotions which often physically manifest themselves. Christ himself told the disabled man at the pool, 'Stop sinning or something worse may happen to you' (John 5 :14), acknowledging the fact that sickness can come as a result of sin.

On the other hand Christ clearly said that not all illness was due to sin. In John 9:2, Jesus' disciples asked Him whose sin had caused the man to be born blind, his own or his parents? Jesus' answer in verse 3 must have revolutionised their thinking - neither sinned, but the healing of his blindness was to bring glory to God. So I concluded some people are sick as a result of sin, some are not. So what about John? He was obviously too young to sin. We struggled with this for some time, desperate for an answer, even hoping the Lord would show us some sin in our own lives that could be put right to allow John healing.

Often, it appeared that God was silent and out of reach when we most needed Him, which put our faith in Him completely to the test. Direction is easier to find when the reasons for the difficult situations in life are clear. But when the answers you're looking for don't come; when you feel absolutely empty and confused; when you're trying to make sense of it all as you search for a distant God, what then? For us, we simply hung on to the promises God gave to His children; promises which He never breaks. We knew He still loved us, not because we always felt that love, but simply because He told us so in His Word, the Bible. I would often pray, 'Lord, despite the fact I can't feel You with me today, I believe You are near, right along side us, simply because You promised You would be.' We had to walk by faith and not by feelings.

We could only surmise that John's illness was for another reason, perhaps, like the blind man, to bring glory to God; but up until that point it had not been made known to us. We are all a part of the human race, subject to suffering and disease whether or not we have put our faith in Christ. The Lord never promised us freedom from pain or trouble, but He did say that He would never leave us nor forsake us, and with our past experience in life, we could testify to that.

In a moment of weakness, when all reason was lost, I looked from John to Dave, swallowed a lump in my throat, and asked him if we had drawn the short straw. 'No, no, we haven't Eleanor,' he said, 'we just don't know why this is happening.' I couldn't afford to let self-pity intrude; John needed us, and he needed us to be strong.

On top of all the worry about our child we found ourselves absorbing the other problems that seemed to constantly arise just to torment us. One such concern was that the SPECT Scan Reports had not arrived from Glasgow. Without them it was unlikely that the operation would take place. Dr Rylance phoned to check they had been posted and was assured they had. My mind was racing. What if they had been lost in the post? The thought of this was unbearable. Or they didn't arrive in time? It seemed we were coming up against one hurdle after another. However, much to everyone's relief, the reports arrived the following morning, the day before surgery. John was transferred temporarily from being under the medical care of Dr Rylance to the neurosurgical care of Mr Walsh and his team.

CHAPTER 8

BRAIN SURGERY
(17th June-23rd June 1992)

It is hard to describe how we felt when we woke on the day our son was going to theatre to have a part of his brain removed. There really wasn't any time for wondering if we were doing the right thing for John. There was no going back. John was not old enough to decide for himself, so we had to trust that by consenting for the operation we were doing the very best for him. But we were churning inside and chattering non-stop with nerves. I wondered at what point I would finally 'break down' and reckoned for me it would be when John was eventually wheeled through the theatre doors - total surrender. How wrong could I be?

Mr Walsh arrived on the ward around 2 pm and had a word with us about the operation. I shared with him that many thousands of people, from various backgrounds (the majority of whom I'd never met) up and down the country, were praying that the Lord would guide his hands. When he responded, 'Let's pray I'm guided to the right spot,' I was full of admiration at his humility.

Meanwhile the nurses were removing from John's forehead the bandage, which had served to hold the ventilator tube in place, in order for the surgeon to have access to shave his head. When I turned round and saw John's dark hair falling onto his forehead, making him look more like himself, I was filled with the deepest emotion imaginable. It was torture not being able to scoop him up and hold him tightly in my arms. I wanted to scream, 'Forget the operation, I'm taking him home.' But all I was capable of was kissing his little face and hands, knowing I must surrender him.

The staff were wonderful and offered to adjust the paraphernalia to allow me the comfort of John in my arms. But I decided against this for fear of disturbing him further. We had opted for the whole of his head to be shaved, as opposed to only the operative site; and, as expected, it altered his whole appearance. The Sister gave me an envelope containing a lock of John's hair - I had already slipped some into my diary - but nevertheless was grateful for a little more to treasure.

When the time came for John to be transferred to theatre it was 'all go', with so much happening at the one time. Doctors, anaesthetists, nurses and porters had their individual roles to play during the transfer from the bed on to the theatre trolley. We were mesmerised, watching the skill of the staff as they disconnected leads from ICU machines and reconnected them to portable ones. Once John was safe on the trolley we were able to be by his side as we accompanied the procession along the corridor to the theatre. Our hearts were racing! When we reached our destination, we were grateful for permission for a quick prayer and a kiss goodbye - then John was gone through the theatre doors. As they snapped shut behind him we were left in an eerie kind of silence, faced with the question: How could we kill five hours?

We walked, talked, prayed, cried, hoped, longed and imagined, before deciding to spend a little while at home with the family. Dave slipped into the college chapel to be alone for a while to seek the help he so desperately needed from the Lord. He chose the side chapel (sacristy) which was smaller and more intimate than the main chapel area and closed over the door to ensure privacy. He lit a candle and, in the silence, quietly begged the Holy Spirit to release the pent-up emotions inside.

Up until this time Dave had always appeared strong and detached from any emotion, but tears soon flowed together with frustration and anger as he poured out his heart to his Creator. 'Why?' he questioned, 'It's so unfair.' As he lifted his head to focus on the candle burning in front of him, he realised there was no movement in the flame which was unusual. From deep within he heard the words: 'This is John, strong and bright and unflickering.' Dave believed this to be the voice of the Lord; he felt a comfort well up inside and a new hope in his heart.

Immediately his anger and fear subsided, leaving such peace and comfort he was able to freely worship and sing praises to Almighty God, grateful for the precious time in His presence. He realised there is no pretence in tears; that the very act of crying is a sign of honesty. When he returned to our home it was evident from his much calmer attitude that he had been able to draw fresh strength and confidence from the Lord.

Several friends popped in to visit us which helped to pass some time. Yet, despite talking about everything and anything, nothing could take our minds off the fact that as our son was on the operating table, his life was severely at risk. We were so relieved to hear over the phone that John had been safely transferred back to ICU. As we drove to the hospital I kept whispering, 'He's alive, he's alive.' When we saw him, he looked anything but so.

I whispered to Dave, 'He looks dreadful.' John lay with his head bandaged, in a maze of drains and drips, with tubes connected to machines; he looked absolutely ghastly, so much so we secretly wondered if it wasn't for the ventilator breathing for him, would he still be alive? He was a deathly shade of yellow and stone cold to touch - his temperature only 25C, the normal is around 36C. Our natural instincts were to immediately warm him up, which the staff encouraged. We each massaged a foot and hand alternately, praying that the heat generated by us would have the desired effect as quickly as possible. Our eyes never left the monitor displaying his temperature; many hours later we eventually saw the fruits of our labour, which allowed the space blanket to be removed, leaving John snug in soft warm covers.

Although exhausted when we reached the parents' block, we were both relieved and grateful the operation was over and prayed that it would prove successful. What we were not aware of at that point was that John was still convulsing.

John looked much better on his first post-operative morning, although it didn't take long before his eyelids showed signs of bruising and swelling, making him look like he'd done twelve rounds in a boxing ring!

The children came to visit with their Grandma. It was too much for Caroline to see her little brother without hair and looking so poorly. She burst out crying and when we asked her if it was because John's head had been shaved, she went on the defensive and assured us it was because she wasn't feeling too well. But each day after that, the first question she would ask was whether John's hair was growing. Louise and David didn't seem to mind being lifted up to give John a kiss; if anything was upsetting them they certainly didn't voice it.

Dave's mother was glad she had been able to stay and see us and John through the operation - she was returning to Newcastle the following day and my parents were arriving from Scotland the same evening. Dave and I were both so fortunate to have such loving and caring parents who willingly helped, in a kind of rota system, to look after their grandchildren. As one set was leaving, the other was arriving; we appreciated everything they did for us.

Dr Rylance paid a social visit with his registrar, Dr Williams, and Dr Akbar, his Senior House Officer. He had such a dry sense of humour and, to break the ice, his first words were, 'I blame the parents!' Of course, as usual, this appealed to us and I quickly gave as good as I got, 'Sorry we can't remove the bandage to show you his earrings!' John did look rather thug-like! We were just relieved the operation was over and enjoyed chatting with the doctors now that we were in a more relaxed frame of mind. We always found Dr Rylance friendly and approachable, which made life easier for us, and we were grateful for the high standard of care we received from him. He looked in on John every day; we appreciated this as we had come to know the medical team so well and felt at ease with them.

A decision was made to commence John on TPN as he was literally fading away before our eyes. Up until then we had never seen him uncovered, but that same day, when we were giving a hand to change his bed linen, I happened to glance up as the nurse quickly exchanged top sheets. For the first time I got a full view of John naked; horrific. 'This can't be John, this can't be my wee son so emaciated.' He looked like a starved child from the Third World. What pain these poor mothers must have to endure in these countries, unable to supply food and milk for their children! Ironically, we had food and milk for John but he was unable to digest it.

So much seemed to happen in the first few days following John's surgery. As soon as the thiopentone infusion was discontinued John showed signs on EEG monitoring of fitting again; so it had to be recommenced. He also required another blood transfusion; his temperature was raised and the amount of oxygen he was receiving had to be increased. We felt we were back to square one and were somewhat downhearted to say the least.

But it was very comforting to hear what was happening at college. The students and staff obviously were grieving with us and were upholding us in prayer. We received many letters and calls, but when word filtered through that they had agreed to give up their morning coffee break to meet in the chapel to pray specifically for John and for us, we were deeply moved. By doing this, apparently many who were often at opposite corners of the classroom, theologically, had grown to respect and love each other in a new way. Barriers had been broken down and in a way a kind of healing had taken place for them. Prayer and concern for our family had brought them together; and that was good.

Many were not only praying for John but were fasting individually as well. Fasting is such a unique discipline with tremendous benefits, not just for the one in need but for the one engaged in it. The abstinence of food, for however long, together with heartfelt prayer, draws the Christian closer to God and deeper into the spiritual realms. This clearer focus when fasting can take place even during the busiest and noisiest day. To learn that men and women were praying and fasting for our little boy released inside me thankfulness and gratitude.

During the couple of weeks John had been in the Intensive Care Unit, we had seen many children come and go. Some went on from strength to strength, whilst others were less fortunate. One such child had been knocked down by a car, sustaining a severe head injury. Following surgery, he fought for his life overnight, but sadly he died the next day. My heart went out to his parents and family and I prayed quietly for strength and comfort to be given to them. At one point I was feeling very vulnerable and actually envied them - *Yes* - envied them. Even though they'd lost their little child; even though they were in deep shock; despite the fact it was so final - I still envied them - they knew where they stood.

In one sense it would have been a relief for us if John had slipped away. The sorrow of the last few months, and more recently the last few days, weighed heavily upon us. Our hopes were constantly raised only to be dashed again. We didn't know at that stage if we were going to lose him anyway; so what was the point of all the months of suffering? Surely anything must be better than this - even death. Such was our agony. Someone actually asked us if we had prepared for John's death. How can you? You can only imagine what it must be like to lose a child, but you can't prepare yourself.

Mr Walsh visited regularly over the weekend, instructing the staff about John's care as necessary. By Monday, after a CT Scan, it was decided that John would need to return to theatre for further surgery. I automatically presumed that John's chance of success would be increased, but to my utter disappointment Mr Walsh could only give us less than a 40% chance. Surgery was scheduled for Wednesday 24th June.

We managed to keep going due to the support we received from staff and friends as well as from my parents. We received numerous phone calls from near and far and were grateful to ICU staff for allowing us access to the telephone in the unit. It helped so often to talk to a friend or relative who was reminding us that they were thinking about us and trying to feel our pain.

One friend commented on how strong I sounded over the phone, much to her relief as she was at a loss what to say. Despite the fact she had been dreading talking to me, she remembers by the end of the conversation feeling that she was the one who had been comforted by my words, instead of the reverse. People were praying for us to be given strength through the ordeal; so perhaps this was evidence of answered prayers. Certainly on one particular occasion, unexpected strength and freedom from the unbearable pain were given instantaneously.

It happened as I was making my way along a corridor to the Intensive Care Unit, with that ever present heavy heart, when suddenly an amazing sensation of 'lightness' empowered me. My sadness was turned to joy and my fears disappeared, leaving me with a conviction that everything was going to turn out fine for John. There was no reason why I should feel like this - John's desperate situation had not altered. Why was I feeling so good? Why was I feeling so strong at this crucial time? As I continued along the corridor, it occurred to me, someone, somewhere, was praying for me.

Many cards and letters poured in from up and down the country. We knew it must have been difficult for people trying to find the appropriate words to say. Yet we were able to take comfort from the sentiments expressed. One such letter from friends in Scotland read:

My Dear David & Eleanor,

Our hearts are heavy when we think of your long battle that you are in with your dear little son. Every hour of every day we think about you all and pray that God, our Father, will give you peace.

It has been such a long time since this all started and we admire your perseverance and faithfulness to God.

· We pray for John's complete recovery, and thank God for a little life that has touched so many people and called them to prayer.

We love you both.

David, Mary and Lucy.

'A little life that has touched so many people and called them to prayer'. If John's little life had brought someone closer to their Creator through prayer, then perhaps it was all worthwhile.

Another letter, sent from a friend in college who had recently visited John, helped to ease the helplessness I was feeling at not being able to do very much for him as a mother. She simply mentioned what a privilege it had been for her to see John 'drinking in' my love. She could see that he was responding to my voice and was enjoying my presence. I needed to hear that. Those words echoed in my mind; 'drinking in Eleanor's love.' What a beautiful way to express John's need for me!

It amazes me how people who claim not to believe in God or His Son Jesus Christ often have a complete change of attitude when trouble strikes. They become more receptive to words of comfort - words which they would have normally considered 'religious'. They talk more about God and respond positively to offers of prayer. Sometimes this has a profound effect on them and they go on to find faith as a result of their trauma. Some, however, once the crisis is over, quickly forget and return to their former ways. Others turn their back on Christianity during a crisis, stating how can God, if there is a God, let these awful things happen to people without intervening. Answers to these questions are not easy to come by; but we must remember that Satan, the enemy of God, is still at work seeking to disrupt and destroy the purpose of God.

I have often wondered how people with no faith in the Lord cope when they are going through troubled waters.

It was our faith in God which was then sustaining us; and when friends managed to reiterate that faith in the following letter we were greatly helped.

Dearest Eleanor,

As God cuddles John in the embrace of His supporting arms, He holds him as if he were a tiny baby; and although in His great strength the burden is light, He feels also the pain and sadness that burdens your heart and Dave's heart; and He knows that His child who is your child is so precious, and He feels with you the heaviness of His charge.

He could not love a child more. Although the hours seem so long to us, they are only like a moment to Him and He is glad to be able to offer you such care because He holds you too. He is gentle as our mothers and strong as our fathers, His kiss breathes life into us all and He seeks to give not take, to comfort and to listen.

When all around John seems so stark and empty, remember that the spaces are filled by God who weeps with you tears that give life, that give us all hope, like dew refreshing the flowers.

He will not leave you.

Our love and prayers as ever,

Paula and Philip.

This letter brought deep spiritual nourishment and helped Dave and I to persevere in the knowledge of our Lord's great love for us and John.

Visitors were allowed in ICU as indeed on the wards and were never made to feel unwelcome, which we appreciated. I remember the College Chaplain, Arnold, visiting John on Ward 6 and offering the sweetest prayer: 'Gentle Jesus, meek and mild, look upon this little child.' The prayer stirred something inside me; something of the tenderness and love Christ has for His little children. In contrast to this, friends also prayed, applying spiritual warfare. So we knew that whatever the outcome with John we had been open to all types of Christian prayer ministry.

Spiritual Warfare?

One woman, who was gifted in the healing ministry, came to pray specifically with Dave and I and to anoint us with oil. We appreciated sharing our hopes and fears together and found a little more assurance which was much needed, but towards the end of the prayers, the evening took on a less serious tone. As she applied the oil to my forehead it immediately started to sting and bite so much that I momentarily lost the thread of the prayer. I was really desperate to lick my finger and rub the stuff off, but not wishing to offend, I suffered in silence. She went over to Dave to repeat the procedure and I couldn't help but chuckle a little to myself as I was unable to pre-warn him of what was ahead. When the prayer was over, I looked across at Dave's bright red forehead; it looked as tender as mine felt! As soon as she had gone, two burning foreheads raced each other to the wash-basin to splash delicate skin with cold water!

A couple who had taken a great interest in John prayed over him on several occasions at home and in hospital. They were troubled at one point and decided to pray over each room in our college flat. When they came to the study they felt there was a spirit of intellectualism present. Dave laughed and said, 'Don't worry, it won't affect me!' Seriously though, we continued to search for reasons for John's illness by the use of spiritual means and felt we had left no stone unturned. We turned no one away who came offering help or advice and tested any 'word' from the Lord that was given to us from fellow Christians. I never really felt completely satisfied with any message given to us, although there was often some element of truth in what was shared. This forced me even further into the arms of Jesus to depend on, and put my complete trust in Him alone.

CHAPTER 9

THEATRE AGAIN
(24th June-28th June 1992)

On Wednesday, 24th June 1992, John was prepared once again for surgery. At 1.50 pm he was transferred to a trolley and we set off on the trek to the theatre suite. I could see a couple approaching as we helped push the trolley up the narrow corridor. We slowed down to make way for them to pass in single file; I shall never forget the look on the woman's face. She leaned over to get a better view of John and, by the expression on her face, wished she hadn't. She immediately shielded her eyes and turned her head away swiftly, visibly showing her disgust. My eyes brimmed with tears at the thought of my flesh and blood repulsing another human being to such an extent. I was about to shout after her, 'He's not an animal!' when Dave, reading the situation, said, 'Never mind, Eleanor, forget it.'

During John's time in theatre Dave and I walked together in the park to gather our thoughts before spending the remaining time in the parents' quarters, resting and waiting. Despite the constant heartache we were suffering, comical situations often arose and helped to lighten our load. We didn't realise it at the time but they were probably a saving force. Who would believe we'd have it in us to laugh when our son was so ill?

One of the toilet doors in the ladies' shower area had been locked for several hours. I knocked and called, but had no reply, so fancying myself as a detective, deduced that someone must be behind the door. Since there were no windows or any space for anyone to get out, it occurred to me that obviously someone had taken ill and needed help. I mentioned it to another parent in the passing but she was hobbling on crutches and made it quite plain she had enough on her plate without getting involved with Sherlock Holmes! I told Dave and we went down to the Reception to report the casualty/corpse? Meanwhile a migraine that had started earlier was now full-blown and I could hardly hold my head up.

By 6.20pm the operation was over. The male nurse looking after John knocked on the door of our room to tell us he was safely back on the unit. Similar to the previous operation, again John looked dreadful, but to our relief seemed to recover more quickly this time. His temperature returned to normal in no time, as did his colour.

As we sat by John's bedside, my head was bursting, and I felt as 'sick as a dog'. But I wanted to be with my son and knew I would not have contented myself back in the parents' room. One of the anaesthetists took one look at me and said, 'Migraine?' He brought me some pain killers and we compared notes on the causes of these dreadful headaches. I hadn't the heart to tell him that this one had been exacerbated by a pseudo-death in the ladies' toilet! Anyone with average intelligence would have considered the possibility of the door blowing shut, securing the lock in place. My next visit to the shower room revealed an open door, an empty toilet and no undertaker!

John's recovery from the second operation ran a similar course to that of his first. A few days later he started to move his left thumb, then he raised his left hand in an attempt to push the ventilator tube out of the way. We hung on to every movement he made and often compared our reaction to the way we felt when our children reached other milestones for the first time. The feeling of pride and joy that wells up when parents see their precious child smile for the first time or say their first word. It was like reliving it all over again, but obviously with a much different emphasis.

Sunday 28th June
Soon John was able to open his eyes and move the fingers of both hands, which delighted us especially since there had been the possibility that he would have a marked weakness or even paralysis down his right side. It was wonderful to feel him grip our fingers and to see his toes move a little. We were beside ourselves with joy and anticipation, but unfortunately by early afternoon the tables once again turned when the EEG result showed fit activity in John's brain.

Before long the fits began manifesting themselves in John's eyes, causing them to bulge and his eyelids to flicker rapidly, to such an extent that they looked like they would at any minute pop out of his head. At the same time his blood pressure rose sky-high; his face, bright red, looked ready to burst. As each episode began, I found myself tensing in fear and whispering over and over again, 'Please stop! Please stop!' Only the day before, everything was going so well; but the contrast now was soul destroying, he seemed to deteriorate so fast. The Registrar prescribed more medication which he hoped would have the desired effect. But there was nothing more that could be done at that point; we could only wait.

To offer a little comfort, the nursing staff had been given permission for me to hold John in my arms at his bedside while they changed his bed linen. Strangely enough I was physically trembling when they placed him on my knee. It had been a few weeks since I'd held him and, being attached to the ventilator, it felt awkward. He immediately started to gag on the tube which distressed him and upset me; so I hastily returned him to bed. The nurse assured me that once the secretions which had gathered at the back of his throat had been cleared, he would settle. Sure as you like she was right.

I cuddled him close to me and, although he was by now more settled breathing-wise, I found it difficult to keep him steady as he continued to jerk erratically. But it felt wonderful, like I was holding him for the very first time. I gripped his little hand and squeezed gently hoping it would help him in some small way to feel secure. Since he had always loved music and singing I decided to sing his favourites to test if he was able to respond at all.

Just for a short while, intermittently, he would rest on me before the movements returned. I stopped singing for a moment and let go of his hand to observe his reaction. It was heartbreaking, watching him struggling to find me. His hand was waving about searching for mine and, although he had very little head control, his head was actually nodding in all directions to find my voice. 'I'm sure he knows I'm here, I'm sure he knows it's me, his mother,' I thought. I cradled and rocked him and sang to him, loving every minute of that precious time. When it was eventually time to return him to bed I was emotionally drained but grateful for having had the unexpected treat.

As soon as Dave arrived I decided to go home for a few hours to see my parents and our children. I shall never forget Caroline's little face when she met me at her bedroom door. She looked up and asked me straight out, 'Is John going to die, Mummy?' My mind was racing as I struggled to find the best way to answer her. Basically I didn't know. I asked her where this idea had come from and she told me the other children at college were talking about it. 'Caroline,' I said, 'I don't really know, darling, but we're all praying to Jesus to make John better. So we've just got to trust Him.' I reminded her that Jesus loves us all so much and that included John, so he was in safe hands. She seemed to understand.

My parents were upset to hear the latest news. It was so difficult for them trying to be strong for our sakes but also needing to express their own grief. A child can go to his parents when in trouble and his parents have that comforting way of making everything alright. This was the exception to the rule. I had a problem, but this time my parents had no power to make it disappear. Yet by talking to them and crying with them that afternoon, that same feeling so familiar from childhood returned.

Simon, a student at college, offered me a lift back to the hospital which I gladly accepted. We arrived just a minute or so after Dave got back from a tea break. I took one look at John and immediately froze. My first impression was that he was dying. 'We're losing our wee son,' I thought. 'Oh God, please, no!' I whispered desperately to myself. A mixture of fear and panic gripped me, and I felt quite nauseated. 'How long has he been like this?' I blurted out. Dave had assured me John had been fine when he had left twenty minutes earlier. John's little eyes were rolling upwards diagonally, and his head gently jerked uncontrollably. His face was extremely pale and he was clammy to touch. This reminded me of patients I had nursed before, who were nearing death. No one knew what to do or say, neither us nor the male nurse looking after John. We just stood staring in silence, in deep shock.

The next I remember, I was sobbing uncontrollably in the hospital chapel, with Simon doing his best to comfort me, whilst Dave could be heard standing his ground with the Sister in charge. She was assuring us that John would not die as he was on a ventilator; but Dave adamantly explained that it was 'brain death' he was concerned about. There didn't seem to be anyone available to make a decision; he was such a difficult case to handle - but we couldn't just sit back and let him die. I contemplated slipping out to a call-box and phoning Dr Rylance at home to make him aware of the situation, hoping he would offer his help, but decided against this.

The Lord had not forsaken John. After all, had He not

promised He would not let his foot slip ... Had He not promised that He would give us back a healthy child? I turned immediately to Simon and pleaded with him to bring someone from Church to pray over John and lay hands on him. He was happy to do this. Dave and I made our way back to John's bedside, terrified at what we might find.

A friend, who worked locally as a GP, visited that evening and could see by our faces and John's deteriorating condition that she had arrived at a crucial time. She sat with us at John's bedside and gave us as much support as she possibly could without revealing her innermost fears. But she told us much later that she honestly felt, going from past experience, that John was dying and had cried herself to sleep that night. She was with us when Simon arrived with the Rev. John Magumba and we all gathered round John's bedside as he read Psalm 46. He prayed for John, then asked if anyone had any oil, as he had left the house in such a hurry he had forgotten to take any. Much to his surprise, I took a little bottle from my handbag (I carry it with me in case a situation warrants its use during prayer) and he lovingly anointed John as he laid his hands on his little head. He prayed once more for his healing ... we could only trust.

John was commenced on a drug called midazolam. It was given to him intravenously via a 'drip' and started at a rate of one millilitre per hour. 'If necessary,' the anaesthetist explained, 'it could be increased to five millilitres per hour.' We had planned to stay up with John all night for fear he might 'slip away', but the anaesthetist advised us to get some much needed rest as we were going to need our strength for the following day. 'We would come to the parents' quarters and get you if an emergency arose,' she reminded us. 'But since John is still on the ventilator he cannot stop breathing.'

She surmised that in the morning the three consultants involved in John's care, i.e. the neurosurgeon, Mr Walsh, the medical consultant, Dr Rylance, and Dr Honisberger, consultant in neurophysiology, would get together and make a decision about John's future. So with these reassuring words we kissed John goodnight and headed for our room. It was difficult to fall asleep as we found ourselves listening to every footstep along the corridor, half expecting it to stop outside our door. We were physically, mentally and emotionally drained, but as Paul writes, 'knocked down, but never knocked out'. We could only leave our precious little son in God's hands. And what safer hands could he be in?

CHAPTER 10

HOPE THROUGH DESPAIR
(Monday 29th June 1992)

As daylight flooded the bedroom on that lovely June morning, the first thought that entered my head was that John must still be holding his own since no one had called us. We had grown accustomed to waking in our room in the parents' quarters without feeling the strangeness we experienced on our first arrival there. On this particular morning, however, my stomach was churning and a mixture of fear and nausea welled up inside as I contemplated the outcome of the day ahead.

I stretched over to the little bedside locker for my Bible knowing that today of all days I was going to need every bit of strength I could possibly muster. Here in my hands was God's Word, God's Word that had transformed many lives in the past; God's Word that had been a saving force to those struggling with painful situations; God's Word capable of meeting my own particular needs even now. But where do I start to look for this relevant passage? It seemed an impossible task until a verse from Psalm 86 came to mind: *Give me a sign of your goodness, that my enemies may see it and be put to shame, for you, O LORD, have helped me and comforted me.*

Unfortunately, although these words had been of benefit some time before, they could offer me no comfort that morning, they just didn't have the hoped-for impact. For some unknown reason I decided to read the full Psalm in reverse order, starting from the last verse, verse 17. I didn't get very far. To my utter amazement words of verse 16 were the most appropriate I could ever have wished to read at that desperate time: *save the son of your handmaiden.*

A tremendous surge of hope welled up inside and permeated my whole being as I meditated on the words over and over again. The Lord Jesus Christ was speaking to me clearly, I had no doubt about that. Coincidence? convince me; Engineered? impossible; Timely? absolutely; Divine guidance? yes! I was the handmaiden, and John, my son, was the one needing to be saved. In these few words I'd been given hope beyond all imagination, hope I intended hanging on to.

Later, Kelvin from the college told me that his wife, Catherine, had felt compelled over that same weekend to pray specifically for me to receive an added measure of faith; her prayer was answered.

Dave listened with interest as I read the verse to him. But I sensed he found it difficult to share my enthusiasm. With the events of the previous day still running through his mind, he feared that John was very close to death. I got up, washed and dressed, and hurried down, as if there wasn't another minute to see my son. Dave said he would follow as soon as he was ready. My heart was racing as I pushed open the doors of ICU and hesitantly approached his bed, not sure what to expect. Although still restless and jerking, he seemed to me a little better. Then my eyes caught the rate to which the midazolam had been increased - double the normal amount! I suspected John had had a rough night and had been difficult to control.

The night nurse looking after John said he'd had a grand mal fit about an hour before. I questioned this to myself, as his erratic movements due to drug withdrawal certainly could have been mistaken for a convulsion. Dave joined me a few minutes later and was disappointed to hear the night nurse's report. When the day staff arrived we decided to take a walk to the children's play area for a breath of fresh air and to gather our thoughts together.

It was a lovely June morning, but unfortunately the sunshine did not reflect our inner emotions. We sat on the bench linking arms; the pain almost too much to bear as we talked and cried. John's illness had never seemed so serious and we both faced, for the first time together, the reality that his death was imminent. We couldn't bear to watch him suffering any longer and felt selfish trying to will him to cling on to life. It was time to let him go, to surrender him to the Lord. Dave prayed, 'Lord, if You must, take John, but please take him soon - don't let him linger any longer.' We felt totally helpless.

My head was swirling with confusion. It seemed the Lord was telling me one thing, but the facts were pointing to something else; and we were leaning more to the facts. Less than an hour before, after receiving those precious words from Psalm 86, I was full of hope for John's healing. So now why were we releasing John into God's care? The mixture of hope and despair continued to torment me for a good part of the day until it finally dawned on me what was happening. I was sure John was going to pull through but the negativity of others left me out on a limb.

On the other hand, the knowledge that if John died he would be at peace forever in the presence of his Creator in heaven, that he would be where love is at its purest, where sickness, crying and pain are banished forever, left me wondering if I should dismiss all hope and accept his dying. But why was I given the verse from the Psalm? *Save the son of your handmaiden.* I just could not give up hope.

Both of us were red-eyed as we made our way back to ICU in plenty of time for the doctors' round. By 9.30 am every child on the unit, bar John, had been seen by their respective doctors. It was a sickening feeling, sitting there by our son's bedside, not knowing why he had been missed. We started to imagine that, because John was proving too difficult a case to handle, the medical staff were avoiding us; otherwise why hadn't John been assessed, as promised the previous evening? We enquired about this to the nursing staff who appeared embarrassed by the situation; but after a few failed attempts by phone to find the reason for the delay, they could only wait patiently with us.

Eventually Dr Rylance appeared with his team and explained there had been a breakdown in communication. The problem now solved, he had been asked to take John again under his medical care. We watched as he spoke to the anaesthetists in charge of ICU, and by their gestures felt we understood a little of what the conversation was about. Dr Rylance looked shocked when he studied John's drug chart and made a few comments to the nurse looking after John.

John was showing involuntary jerking type movements in his shoulders, arms and legs. His lower jaw continually moved horizontally from right to left, giving the impression he was constantly chewing. His eyes couldn't focus at all and kept rolling around in all directions whilst he constantly salivated. I knew he could hear, as my voice seemed to soothe him momentarily before the restlessness would return. Dr Rylance agreed with me that John's present behaviour was due to drug withdrawal and not to convulsions.

The Hard Truth

He knew it was time to discuss John's future and called us into an available room in ICU along with his Registrar and House Officer. The Sister in charge of the unit together with the nurse looking after John joined us also and the door of the small office was closed, creating an air of seriousness. Swallowing was difficult as we settled into our seats. We already had a rough idea about what we were going to be told, but when the time came to finally hear it we were shaken out of our numbness and forced to face reality.

Dr Rylance broke the uncomfortable silence by saying how disappointed he was to learn that John had started fitting again and shared with us the conversation he'd had with the anaesthetists earlier on. It was more or less as we had surmised. They had felt it would not be worthwhile starting John on thiopentone again as he'd been on and off it for over three weeks without any respite to the fitting. Dr Rylance, on the other hand, was of the opinion that if John was given this drug continually for five days without interruption, it might possibly control his seizures.

He asked our opinion and Dave immediately responded by wondering whether such treatment would only prolong the agony? This took Dr Rylance aback slightly. He was quick to share with us that normally parents are begging him to do his utmost to prolong their child's life, but here we were almost willing to surrender John without a fight. Together we explained that we could not watch John suffering any longer, and to have him 'knocked out' again, with no guarantee of success, only to face him going through a kind of 'cold turkey' mingled with fits at the end of it all, seemed unbearable. He insisted, however, that there was a chance of success and advised us to take it, which naturally we agreed to.

We were moved when he took time to enquire why we were not showing any signs of anger in our present situation, either towards God or towards the staff, since he believed we had every right to. In reply, I said, 'Dr Rylance, I've loved the Lord for many years and although I don't understand why God is allowing this to happen to John, I can't be angry. Confused and devastated, yes, but not angry. When my fiance was killed it was like being in a kind of hell, but at least I knew where I stood. I had to face it. But this, this is like some kind of torture, not knowing if John's going to live or die. Nevertheless I can't be angry.' He accepted this straightaway and continued explaining his plan for John.

He first of all wanted to reverse the drug midazolam to find out if it was responsible for holding the fits at bay, or if the present fit free period was indeed due to surgery. He would do this under EEG monitoring. If John remained fit free after the midazolam was reversed, then he would stay on his present anti-convulsant regime, but if he showed signs of fitting then he would immediately go back on thiopentone. After five days he would be slowly weaned off the drug and ventilator. Afterwards, John would either live or die. So it seemed we would need to talk about the possibility of John dying. The expression on my face must have revealed my thoughts. There must be some mistake; this just can't be happening.

I summoned the strength to ask him what eventually would cause John's death, but found myself mentally blocking his explanation; the pain of visualising John dying, too much to bear. I put my head down on the desk and started sobbing uncontrollably, 'He's my wee boy, he's my wee son. Oh, God, help me please; please help me.' All eyes were focused on the floor and there was a deathly silence for the few minutes it took for me to pull myself together. Dr Rylance was staring straight ahead, his eyes moist with tears ... I asked him to promise me that John wouldn't suffer, that he'd die peacefully ... he gave me his word ... there was nothing more to be said ...

As we headed back along the corridor, friends from church were waiting to see us and their visit couldn't have been more timely. By this time Dave and I were so distraught we had to be taken to the hospital chapel to be

113

consoled. It was so hard for them to know what to say; but what I remember was Sarah crying with me as she held me tightly in her arms, and Cedrick with his arm around Dave, who in all the time I had known him, had never seemed so heartbroken. He was sobbing like a child who could not be comforted. I actually feared that he would 'snap'.

Aware of someone sitting behind us in the chapel, I turned round to see Kate, the Hospital Chaplain, praying quietly. Immediately my mind flashed back to something I'd been thinking about only a few days before: communion. We never gave our children communion, preferring to wait until they were mature enough to understand the seriousness and power of that beautiful sacrament.

I remember one day gazing at John lying so 'far gone', fearing that I might never see him conscious again. I imagined him running up and down and calling to us until the pain made me ache deep within, to the extent that I thought I would go mad if we couldn't have our wee boy back again, back to his old self. If a child has been given a short time to live, the immediate reaction of his parents is to spoil him in as many ways imaginable. It's an attempt to give him as full a life as possible, providing of course he is physically able to cope with it. Fun fairs, cinemas, shows, holidays, anything to bring pleasure whilst his days are numbered.

But here we were, deprived of even that. We talked to John and sang to him, but we had no way of proving that he could actually hear us now, or feel the love that was pouring from us. Since we couldn't take John anywhere to give him the time of his life, what did we have left, if anything, as parents to offer? What would be the very best thing we could give him under the circumstances?

John Receives Communion

Immediately I had thought of communion. What else could be more fulfilling; more enriching; more powerful; more precious than communion? Communion with the living Christ. We knew John could not receive the bread, the body of Christ, but his lips could be moistened with the wine - the blood of Christ - blood that was shed on the cross for mankind, including John. By His stripes we are healed ... by His stripes John can be healed.

When I looked round at Kate I thanked the Lord for His timing and for bringing communion to mind once more. She told us later that she had been desperate to give John communion but didn't mention it for fear of forcing her opinion on us.

It was a fairly short, but beautiful service. Sarah, Cedrick, Dave, Kate and I gathered round John's bedside which was still screened to allow some privacy. Dave cried the whole way through and had no control to join us when we quietly said 'The Lord's Prayer' together. I, on the other hand, felt triumphant and full of expectation, especially when Kate said, *'John, the Blood of Christ.'* The peace and power of God seemed to permeate John's whole being. Something supernatural had taken place.

Sarah and Cedrick took Dave home at lunchtime so

that he could have a break and let family members know the situation. I suggested to him that we tell no one about the morning's events as I was becoming weary of sharing the latest news of John, only to have the whole story change dramatically in a matter of hours. But Dave insisted that we put family and friends in the picture. My parents were heartbroken, and so were Dave's when he phoned them in Newcastle to ask them to come down to Birmingham straightaway. He phoned relatives and friends in Scotland, but grief overwhelmed him, forcing him to hang up without completing his conversations.

Once he'd gathered himself together, he took a walk in the college grounds, his thoughts dominated by John. 'I'll never kick a ball with him here again,' he thought. It was hard for Dave to keep up as he shared the news of John with students he met in the passing. He finally broke down again and headed for the chapel. There he lit a candle once more, and as he watched the flame rise, he heard the words for a second time, 'This is John, strong and bright and unflickering.' 'Yes, Lord,' he reasoned, 'in heaven.' He was totally convinced we were soon to lose our son and that his healing would come through his death.

Meanwhile I was at John's bedside, aware that the news had spread like wildfire around the hospital. Members of staff obviously knew about the situation, but were understandably feeling awkward and didn't know what to say to me. Some just whispered, 'I'm sorry to hear about John.' Others said it all with a touch. Friends from college, Joy and Paula, arrived to give their support, when the news of John's deterioration filtered through to there. It must have been so awkward and difficult for them to know how to act and what to say. But at a time like that words are useless. Parents in such situations are not looking for others to spout forth great words of philosophy because quite frankly, unless they have experienced the imminent death of a child, they cannot begin to understand the pain. What I needed was someone to hold me in their arms and simply cry with me. Not to reduce what we were experiencing with empty words - just someone to cry with me.

Joy and Paula struggled to find something appropriate to say as they walked with me to the playground for a break. As soon as we reached the bench and sat down I immediately wanted to be back at John's bedside. I couldn't concentrate or content myself for any length of time and was acting like someone demented, which left them wondering how to handle it. The agitation continued for hours. At his bedside I wanted to be away; when apart from him, I wanted to be back to hold his hand.

At one point, everyone seemed to be writing John off which stirred a little anger in me. I looked at one of the nurses and said, 'Am I wrong to have hope for John?' He put his arms around me and said, 'A little while ago I would have answered, "yes," but I see a slight improvement in him now, so don't give up.' I could have kissed him. One of the other nurses was passing and asked if I was OK. 'Margaret,' I said, 'I can't help feeling this hope that John is going to make it.' She answered so caringly, 'Hang on to that if it's what you believe.'

When Dave returned from home, I decided to go back

with Paula and Joy. I was dreading seeing my parents as I felt in some strange way responsible for causing their present pain. David Parker, who had baptised John, was spending some time with them when I arrived. I immediately threw my arms round my mother and burst out, 'Mam, he's my wee boy.' My father cuddled me, then he himself started sobbing. Can you drown in grief? We came pretty close. David took my hand in his and spoke words of comfort, but my blank mind was incapable of absorbing any detail. I did sense, however, that he was trying to be strong for us as he shared our agony.

He offered a lovely prayer and then said he would go to the hospital to give some support to Dave. Dave appreciated this, and they walked to the playground where they sat for most of the time in silence. When Dave did feel like talking, David listened sympathetically and they also prayed together.

Later I returned and joined Dave at John's bedside. Dave shared that he had noticed a brightness in John's eyes that he hadn't seen up until then. He held his little hand as he said, ' He's not gone yet.' Now we both had hope and that was good. We eventually went for a cup of tea in the parents' dining area which was empty when we sat down. We felt sick. By this time, we had become accustomed to ordering food and drink only to realise we hadn't the appetite for it when it was placed in front of us.

A Vietnamese woman whose daughter had suffered a stroke sat down opposite to us. Glancing over and recognising us she came and stood by our sides. She laid one hand on Dave's arm and the other on mine and squeezed gently. I shall never forget that touch. She had no words to say but just a look on her face that portrayed sympathy and understanding - it was then that we realised word of John's deterioration had reached the ward. Eyes brimming with tears she returned to her cup of tea in silence. We had found a common bond. Suffering is universal.

Dave's parents were arriving in the evening from Newcastle, so I stayed at John's bedside while Dave met them at the station. Our meeting was emotional, though each was trying to be strong for the other. We didn't broach the subject of John's prognosis, but they had come expecting to attend his funeral. They were shocked when they saw just how ill John was and how much weight he had lost, but were grateful to be by our sides to offer all the love and support they could.

Many cards and letters were waiting for us when we arrived home that evening. While my mother and father were welcoming Dave's parents, I opened one letter after another and understood the struggle friends and family members had, trying to find appropriate words to say at this desperate time. Some of them displayed a little anger with God for allowing this to happen. They reasoned that we had given up so much to answer a call to the ministry, but instead of receiving blessings we were faced with what appeared to be on the outside, frank opposition; they just couldn't make the connection.

I honestly never saw it like that. In life, joys and heartaches weave their way along our path whether we are in His service or not. He causes His sun to rise on the evil and the good, and sends rain on the righteous and the unrighteous (Matthew 5:45). One thing was for sure, that despite the fear and struggle with John, a sustaining peace had remained throughout. The peace that really does pass all understanding. Not the relaxing, free from trouble, everything is going well, peace; but the inexplicable peace that arises from the knowledge that the Saviour, through each emergency, was standing there with us, sharing the load.

As I continued to open the mail, the contents of one envelope were so unexpected that it took me a little by surprise to say the least. It simply contained a poem; a poem that moved us deeply and one which I knew I would treasure for the rest of my life even if the outcome with John was not favourable. It had been written by Allison Marriot, a student at Queens. She will never know what it meant to us, nor the gratitude we felt towards her for taking the time to compose such a poignant piece of work.

Johnny those eyes of yours are dancing in my heart
Johnny that hand of yours curling soft and pale
Is clinging to my fingertips and gliding through my soul
Johnny that hair of yours darkening, strong and free
Is waving on my lap tonight, Johnny, can you see?

Can you see how much I love you?
Can you see how much I care?
Can you see how much I worry?
When I'm screaming, Don't you dare!

Johnny, put the scissors down!
John - get off the chair!

120

John - come back in here!
You'll be falling down the stair!
John, let's change that nappy,
John, let's brush your hair,
John, lie you down to sleep,
Shush Johnny, not a sound.
Johnny, close those eyelids
Shut out those orbs of brown
Johnny snuggle badger-like beneath the eiderdown....

Johnny can you see me?
Can you see how much I care?
Do you know how much I love you
When I'm screaming, Don't you dare?

Johnny those eyes of yours are dancing in my heart,
Johnny, that hand of yours, soft and small and smart,
Johnny, that hair of yours is oh, so strong and free
Johnny, Johnny, Johnny, Johnny, can you see?

It was so descriptive of the John we knew and loved, the John we wanted back again and it really captured the mischievous side of him. In addition, the connotations running through the poem were incredible; they took us alternately from what had been back to the present.

'Don't you dare!' were words frequently used when John was well and running around, especially if he was about to get up to something he knew he shouldn't. He would look round waiting for us to reprimand him in our usual slow and deliberate tone, 'Don't ... you ... dare!' This always made him laugh, and of course amused us also as he attempted to repeat the performance. But over the last few days, as time appeared to be running out, I'd

121

been screaming inside, 'Don't you dare - die. Don't you dare.' I remember whispering in his ear, 'Fight this, John, you've got to fight it, darling.'

We were missing so much the normal routine care of John portrayed so aptly in the fourth stanza, and found it painful to dwell on it in case we would never experience the joy of caring for him again and having him at home, a part of the family. We would have done anything to have the old John back again, sitting on our knee, brushing his hair, telling him a story, hearing his voice and seeing his smile.

The poem throughout, although bitter-sweet, was powerful, reaching a climax with that final question, posed with such desperation, Johnny, Johnny, Johnny can you see? These words held the fear, the frustration and the pain that was tearing us apart. We were pleading inside to know if he could see us, if he could hear our voices and feel our touches that caressed him with everything we had. There are instances of unconscious patients who after recovery can recall every word that was spoken by their bedside. With this in mind we talked to John, believing he could hear and understand our every word.

I remember looking at him one day and praying, 'Lord, if You bring John round just enough for him to know who we are and to be aware that we love him dearly, then we won't ask for anything else.' And I meant it. This was perhaps me hoping that John would not need to suffer any more and we could just spend the time loving and caring and protecting him and making up for lost time.

I often wondered just what he'd thought of us when we so often had to help hold him down as the doctor approached with yet another needle. 'How can you let them do this to me, Mam? You're even helping them!' It seemed that these weren't his thoughts because after the trauma was over John would smile and respond to a cuddle before leaping off my knee and returning to play.

I shared the poem with Dave and the family who were equally moved. I had to see Allison to thank her for writing it and let her know just how much the words had meant to me. When she opened the door all I could do was sob, 'Oh Allison.' She just held me in her arms and cried with me. I was grateful for that. She seemed to know at that point that words were futile. When I gathered myself together, we chatted and cried over a cup of tea as I shared the day's events with her.

Dave and I returned late to the hospital and stayed overnight at the parents' quarters, but this time a little hope had filtered through and we were determined to cling on to it.

I was under the impression that my prayer entered in the book that day, which read *Help us Lord, Amen, Dave and Eleanor* must surely be one of the shortest written, until I came across the most heart-rending prayer. It simply read, *Father, Why?*

Only two words, but two words that spoke volumes. There was no signature to identify the writer, or enough information to reveal the problem. *Father, Why?* Why what? Why is my child ill? or Why my child? or Why did my child die? Here was someone tying up the agony and pain and despair and hurt they were experiencing in this short prayer; desperate for answers which might help make sense of it all; someone who needed reasons for the suffering; someone who felt very helpless. How could two words say so much? But they did. How can so many parents identify with them? But they can.

The ever controversial issue of transplants remained at the forefront of our thoughts during our vigil by John's bedside. We had time, and plenty of it, to explore all aspects including the ethical implications involved in organ donation and transplant. We wanted to make up our minds one way or another, a very difficult and painful task, and although reaching our final decision to offer John's organs, we hoped it would never come to that. Much later the procedure for the removal of the organs was explained to us.

No doubt many parents and relatives have the satisfaction of knowing that through the loss of their loved one, another has received the healing they've been so desperate for, through organ transplant. A sense of something good coming out of all the pain, but could we have said goodbye to John still 'breathing' on a ventilator? Could we? Thank God that decision was taken out of our hands.

With Dave training for the ministry, it wasn't uncommon for us to receive visits from clergy of various denominations who had heard of our plight. It said a lot for them, coming into the hospital and seeking out a couple and their child whom they had never met before. One afternoon a minister arrived in Intensive Care wearing a sheepish kind of sympathetic smile as he glided into the department, almost as if he was on a skate-board with someone working him by remote control! He had heard how seriously ill John was and had come to offer us as much support as he could.

I was feeling rather agitated and easily irritated that particular day, and quite frankly had to admit that this minister, for no reason, was getting up my nose. He had arrived at the wrong time, that's all, so he unfortunately was the one who was going to 'catch it'. I'm normally a very tolerant person but it took me all my time not to scream, 'Stop creeping in as if you've no right to be here; and speak up instead of muttering and mumbling; and stop trying to be nice.' The pressure of the last few days and weeks was obviously now starting to take its toll. Perhaps we were getting tired of sympathy, I don't know, but still that was no excuse for almost snubbing the clergyman! He turned out to be one of the loveliest persons I had ever met which left me feeling quite ashamed of myself. (But he did look as if he was being worked by remote control!)

CHAPTER 11

ANOTHER CHANCE
(30th June-20th July 1992)

It seemed when Tuesday arrived that John's life was being held in the balance. I was at his bedside, holding his hand, loving and caring for him in the way only a mother can. Dr Rylance arrived on the unit early. He came over to my side and laid his hand on my shoulder tenderly. 'How are you coping, Mrs Hall?' It went without saying that I was obviously anxious and uptight on this, one of the most important days of John's young life, but I was there in the thick of it ready to face the result, whatever it might be.

Dave's parents sat by their grandson whilst I stood at the other side of the bed. The EEG technicians attached the leads to John's scalp in preparation for the procedure. We had come to know the technicians well, as the number of EEG's John eventually had totalled 32 - a hospital record apparently! They often shared a comforting word with us and were more than sympathetic and supportive now.

John received the first injection from Dr Hall to reverse the drug midazolam. As the paper tracing the brain patterns unfolded from the machine, I took a sharp intake of breath. To my untrained eye it looked horrendous with lots of heavy zig zag lines which seemed to have gone haywire - John must still be fitting, I feared. We all waited in anticipation for Dr Honisberger to give the result, which surprisingly was clear. The crazy pattern had appeared as a result of interference due to John's continual jerking and movement and was not indicative of any fits. When I looked over at Dave's mother, tears were rolling down her cheeks with relief - I knew she and his father were silently praying, and praying like they'd never done before.

It was still early days as the reversal of the drug required two further injections. Yet it was looking a little more hopeful.

After the second injection I put my lips close to John's ear and sang some of his favourite songs whilst grasping his little hand. It was remarkable to see how this had a most calming effect on him, as he stopped fidgeting to concentrate on my voice. This was reflected quite clearly on the monitor when much to our delight a less erratic trace unfolded. Again Dr Honisberger gave the 'all clear'. We were frightened to say too much but each found it hard to suppress the hope welling up inside. This was plain to see on each of our faces as worried looks gave way to sudden smiles.

Two down and one to go! The result of the final injection and trace was as favourable as the previous ones and brought such joy it was hard to contain - we were beaming. This meant John would not require any further thiopentone and could now be left to 'come round' in his own time. Of course he wasn't out of the woods yet, but we could not have asked for better results. I was desperate to tell Dave and my parents the good news - I felt like shouting it from the roof tops - JOHN'S NOT FITTING NOW.

Dave, alone in the parents' quarters, had been spending some time in prayer and meditation. When he came across Psalm 91 he knew instantly the Lord had given it to him for John. As he read it over and over again it seemed that every aspect of the psalm had implications solely for John.

There was first of all a 'thread of protection' running throughout - protection which John desperately needed: 'He will cover you with his feathers, and under his wings you will find refuge' (verse 4); 'They (the angels) will lift you up in their hands so that you will not strike your foot against a stone' (verse 12).

The saving force spoke strongly: 'Surely he will save you from the fowler's snare and from the deadly pestilence' (verse 3); 'I will rescue him; I will be with him in trouble' (verses 14, 15). John was certainly in trouble and here was a promise of help to cling on to.

The final verse held the key words for Dave: 'With long life will I satisfy him and show him my salvation.' He believed strongly that this promise was for John, and felt that we had at long last reached a definite turning-point. Through this psalm he received fresh hope that not only was John going to pull through, but he would enjoy long life! Any former doubts vanished and from there on Dave had a new confidence which was evident when we spoke together. He was delighted with the EEG result and saw it as final confirmation of all that had transpired that morning.

Because John's behaviour resembled convulsions, a

video tape was made to record his movements, whilst simultaneously, an EEG tracing was captured also on video. Being normal, this was proof that John was not fitting and served to help the nursing staff distinguish between proper grand mal fits and movements that were the result of drug withdrawal.

During the morning's events, John's little friends on Ward 6 had been working hard making a giant get-well card for him under the guidance of Gayle, the Play Therapist. The card, gorgeous and full of imagination, was designed in such a way that when it was opened, a frog appeared to leap out from the centre. When I saw it in pride of place on the shelf behind John's bed and read the get-well message from the children, I felt the warmth of love and compassion it conveyed so uplifting. Others were sharing the joy that today's good news had brought, and that was special.

Over the next two days, the Hospital Chaplain gave John communion at our request. We believed that when he was anointed and first received the wine it was the turning-point for John and that through this sacrament God was working a miracle. It also served to remind us that if everything was being done for John physically through the hands of the medical staff, then how much more was being done for him spiritually through the hands of God, his loving heavenly Father?

By Wednesday morning John had been taken off the ventilator for the first time in several weeks and was breathing confidently by himself into an oxygen mask. We were amazed at how smoothly this had gone; absolutely no complications. After having the ventilator tube in position for so long we expected him to be a little hoarse, but when he coughed, we got the surprise of our lives to hear him sounding just like Donald Duck! Bless him, we did hope his vocal chords weren't as raw and painful as they sounded.

He was transferred into a single cubicle in ICU and made comfortable there. Despite his continual restlessness it was a pleasure to watch him breathe by himself, free from the ventilator. Dr Rylance was marvellous and paid many visits throughout the day, adjusting John's medication as blood results warranted, and generally supporting us as a family. He was trying to keep everything on a low key but we found it hard to contain our joy - especially Dave's parents! Dr Rylance asked me to try and calm Dave's mother down as the day's events had left her over-excited. After all, they had at long last wakened from their nightmare and could return to Newcastle with freer minds, so who was I to dampen their elation?

Mr Walsh visited John on Wednesday evening and enquired after him. He could see I was pleased with his progress, but I sensed by the expression on his face that he didn't share my enthusiasm. He took a look at John, then asked to see his drug chart before bidding us a good evening. With these few words, he made a hasty retreat out of the door, leaving me rather confused at his sober manner. It turned out that when he saw John he actually thought he was still in status and felt at that point there was absolutely no hope for him. Dr Rylance later assured him that the EEG monitoring showed the contrary, much to Mr Walsh's surprise and relief.

That night John had only about ten minutes sleep altogether! He continued to jerk and chew in a restless manner and constantly salivated like a young baby. His voice still resembled Donald Duck when he coughed, so we expected it to take a few days before it would improve. He was opening and closing his mouth, as if attempting to talk, but no sound came out. I wondered what he himself made of it all, but we shall never really know.

The next day he had the stitches from his head removed, leaving a dry, clean wound; since being taken off the ventilator, his observations had been satisfactory so he was disconnected from the heart monitor; he had another clear EEG once again, much to our relief. I happened to comment on how sticky his scalp had become with the special gel used by the EEG Technicians, when to my surprise the Sister said, 'Well, let's give him a bath,' and sent the nurse to collect the necessary equipment. It sounded like a good idea although I felt a little apprehensive, as though we were rushing him on.

The air conditioning in the department had broken down and was blowing cooler air than normal. After only a few minutes in the bath John started to shiver and 'croak' in disapproval. This tore at my heart as I knew he wasn't enjoying the experience and needed to be wrapped up in a soft, warm towel and held tightly. At that point I wished I'd never mentioned the stickiness on his scalp. After coming this far I hoped the bath wouldn't be detrimental to him, as he was still a sick child. Instinct, rightly or wrongly so, told me to keep him quiet and warm and to speak and sing softly to him; not to put him through what must have seemed like an ordeal. The Sister in charge was so overjoyed at John's miraculous recovery (as indeed the rest of the staff on the unit were) that she sent the nurse for the polaroid camera to take a photo of John in his bath. I would have preferred them to make him more comfortable but was actually grateful in the end to have the picture as we were later able to compare it with other photos and see his progress.

Two nurses from Ward 6 popped in to visit John, so I was able to thank them for the beautiful display of flowers that we had received from all the staff on the ward. They had been so happy for us when they heard the encouraging news that they decided to send us flowers, together with their well wishes. Because this gesture was so unexpected and away from the 'done thing' it brought us tremendous amount of pleasure.

Each hour we watched for signs of improvement in John. The Play Therapist, Helen, hung a mobile from the ceiling and we were heartened to note how it periodically caught his eye. He was tolerating sips of juice and appeared to know our voices. To us, John looked so much better, but by the expression on the faces of those who hadn't seen him for a number of weeks, he looked drastic. Some of them found the experience too painful and only stayed a matter of minutes, for fear of upsetting us.

Back To The Ward
On Thursday 2nd July, 1992 John was discharged from

ICU. A lot of water had gone under the bridge since he'd first been admitted there. Who would have believed that only a few days after all hope was nearly lost for him, he would be back in the ward? One of the Nursing Sisters said she honestly believed that some of the children got better *despite* what they did for them and not because of *what* was done for them. This seemed true in John's case. Children with the same diagnosis can receive the same treatment and yet the outcome can vary remarkably - some go on to make a full recovery whilst others less fortunate lose their lives. It is quite obvious there is something else at play, and it is not of a physical nature.

It was a wonderful feeling packing up John's bits and pieces ready for the move to the ward. There were plenty of hugs and smiles all round and well wishes for the future as the staff said goodbye and waved us off. But after the hustle and bustle of the transfer, my mood changed dramatically when I found myself alone with John for the first time in many weeks. As he continued to jerk and twitch, apparently unaware of his surroundings, his whole future seemed to pass quickly in my mind. How would I manage to cope if this was to be the John we would be left with? When he was at death's door I had promised to be content if we could have him back conscious and recognising us, and that still stood. But in the silence, the silence that disturbed rather than nourished, I wondered if I had the disposition, the temperament or the compassion to love and support my child for the rest of his life, if he remained as he was at present, mentally and physically disabled.

The physiotherapist soon interrupted my thoughts when she brought John a special chair which was ideal in meeting his particular needs. She showed us and the nursing staff several ways to position John to make him more comfortable. These included crossing his arms and tying his wrists together which was effective in controlling some of the jerking movements and making him feel more secure; and placing pads behind his shoulders.

To test his awareness a little, I played a 'Fireman Sam' video and watched his reaction. To my amazement, he managed to struggle with his erratic head movements, and followed the direction of the sound, until he was eventually facing the screen. He seemed to calm momentarily as he listened to the familiar voices, but the involuntary movement of his eyes prevented him from focusing on the picture. We were getting through and that was all that mattered.

John had gone all of Wednesday and Thursday with only a few minutes sleep, so by Friday we were starting to feel quite concerned and asked Dr Rylance if he could possibly sedate John. He was reluctant to do so, understandably, considering the amount of medication John had had recently, but assured us he wouldn't come to any harm. Much to our relief he slept soundly throughout Friday night and was so much the better for it the next morning. He sat in his chair which had been secured high on his bed, and waved to Mavis the ward domestic. This was certainly encouraging and cheered us no end.

The other children on the ward were delighted to have John back amongst them and made such a fuss of him. They took it in turn to have their pictures taken with him, which we were happy to allow, although I was a little annoyed to arrive at the ward one day to find John being pictured without a hat. I felt as though by photographing him with his head shaven and bearing a huge scar was in a strange kind of way exposing him. But I quickly realised that children accustomed to hospital wards accepted each other as they were, and very rarely noticed physical differences obvious to outsiders. So cameras clicked and children posed and it made very little difference to them whether friends had tubes up their noses or coming out of their ears! For them this was the norm; for them no need to be in best dress; for me, this was very humbling.

John continued to improve over the next few days and was managing a very light diet. His food and fluid chart one day proudly read: *ONE CHIP!* much to the amusement of many. He was, however, going to need many more chips if he was to regain the weight he'd so drastically lost. (He was a mere 9.9 kgs - just over 21 lbs.) But over the next fortnight it was a pleasure to watch him being steadily built up, with his daily weigh-in becoming one of the highlights of the day! He became more aware of his surroundings, his erratic movements improved and he was able to hold some toys.

The medical staff were delighted with his progress and kept a watchful eye on him. During one of the ward rounds, Dr Williams was examining the 'S' shaped wound on his head when Dave said, 'It looks like a tennis ball.' Dr Williams replied, 'Well let's hope he bounces back!' Slick, and we loved it. We were always ready for some humour and appreciated this latest offering!

Is The Dream Over?

Tuesday, 7th July sounded like a record we'd all heard over and over again. John was fitting again. One of the ICU nurses had popped in to visit John to find out how he was doing. He was fast asleep as we stood at his bedside chatting. During our conversation I glanced at John's face and thought I detected a slight flicker of his eyelids. 'It can't be,' I thought, but soon he was twitching and it was plain to see he was in a fit.

How can I describe my reaction to a situation that destroyed my so-recent elation? Devastated? Demoralised? Desperate? Words cannot express the pain we felt that day or the thoughts that tortured our minds. Was John starting all over again? Dr Rylance came immediately to the ward when the news reached him. He commented on how well he felt I was coping although I'm sure he sensed my agony. I often wondered how he must have felt during each crisis, having to make difficult decisions for John and counsel us at the same time; not a job to be envied; but he always took the situation in hand and showed such compassion. We had developed a deep trust and confidence in him and knew that with John in his care we could not ask for more.

The following day it was all behind us and from then on, John went from strength to strength. He started saying single words like 'tea' and 'Dad' and over the following weeks extended his repertoire greatly. He was able to hold and drink from a cup and was eventually eating a normal diet. His artificial feeding was reduced and finally discontinued under the guidance of the dietician.

John enjoyed walks to the playground in the buggy and became more alert each day. On one such outing from the ward I had stopped for a drink and was sitting opposite the parents' tearoom when suddenly a woman came rushing up the corridor screaming for her husband. I caught the gist of the emergency. Her son had collapsed unexpectedly and the doctors were working with him to save his life. I felt nauseated and prayed desperately for the child and the family but unfortunately they lost their little son. What can you say? What can you do? It felt then - very little. In an illogical way, because of this experience, I had a feeling of guilt, as if we had no right to have John alive. Why was our son saved and not hers? These unanswerable questions often tortured and dampened our joy.

John was allowed home for a few hours on a couple of occasions, before his final discharge from hospital. There was plenty of excitement in our home and around the college when he arrived. Paula made him a special cake in the shape of a train, with carriages loaded with sweeties. There was such a sense of joy and happiness and I'm sure that, although he was unable to express it verbally, he thoroughly enjoyed being home again.

To cap it all, young David asked me so innocently, 'Does that mean Johnny belongs to us now?' He had missed his brother so much, especially since they shared a bedroom, and had obviously got it into his head that John was hospital property since he'd been away for so long. 'Does that mean Johnny belongs to us now?' The words lingered in my mind as I realised the question was saying much, much more. Fortunately I could allay all those fears by my simple answer, 'Yes!' Louise burst out one night full of excitement, 'Oh I just can't wait for John to come home for good and sleep in his own cot.'

Finally Discharged

When John did come home for good we had a special party for him and invited all the children from college. They gave him little home-made 'welcome home' cards and made such a fuss of him that we can honestly say it was a day to remember. It was a time for rejoicing; for thanking God for the miracle; a wonderful day.

Before leaving the ward, many of the hospital staff came to wave goodbye to John. Plenty of snapshots were taken and promises made to keep in touch. There was such a sense of friendship and love and probably most of all - *relief!* We had come a long way since his first admission - *a very long way*.

It was wonderful to have John home amongst his family again; there was a feeling of newness which was mingled somehow with a little apprehension on our part. It took several nights before we were able to relax completely as initially we felt vulnerable, with no immediate backup should anything go wrong. But as the days became weeks we eventually gained enough confidence to cut down on our many 'trips' during the night to his bedroom to check that he was sleeping peacefully.

CHAPTER 12

RECOVERING AT HOME
(21st July–31st December 1992)

Just doing the ordinary things in life brought such joy. John seemed so pale after being cooped up in hospital, so to see him sitting in the college garden soaking in the sunshine was marvellous. Mind you, sitting was not the operative word. John wanted to be on the go and needed plenty to amuse him. He had been loaned a special Jenna chair from the physiotherapy department which was designed in such a way as to support him completely. The tray in front prevented him from falling forward and the foot rests were adjustable allowing his feet to be positioned at right angles. Technically, the chair was safe, but with John being a typical lad and full of spirit it didn't take him long to discover that he could rock backwards and forwards; a dangerous occupation, so we had to jam the chair against the wall for safety.

He seemed to enjoy walks in his buggy more than ever and took in everything around him as though he was seeing it for the first time. It seemed that together we were discovering the beauty of nature all over again, and I wondered just how much he remembered and how much was 'new' to him. On the way home from one such outing my heart went out to him. Our children were flocking round showing him leaves and berries they'd found along the way. They were pointing to squirrels and aeroplanes, and anything that they thought would interest him, when suddenly he let out a piercing scream. I caught sight of a wasp escaping from the group and realised that he had been stung. And what a length of a sting. I was able to pull it out of his arm with my fingers. A little anger arose in me - why John? Not that I would have wished any of our other children to have been on the receiving end, but hadn't John had enough? Fortunately he was none the worse for it.

Over the following weeks John made steady progress. He attended physiotherapy three times a week and was seen regularly in the outpatient department by Dr Rylance. He was still only able to crawl but could pull himself up to stand, which compared with a baby of about ten months. In addition, he was saying single words and was able to feed himself. One gift which returned quickly was his ability to sing. We often sang familiar songs to him, deliberately missing out some words to encourage him to respond. We were delighted to hear him complete the missing gaps, right on key and right on time! We couldn't agree more with the doctor who said that John had an amazing musical aptitude. His ability to remember melodies was incredible for a child of his age.

I remember one of the appointments John had with the consultant after his discharge. Dr Rylance, when introducing us to his new Registrar, said, 'Meet John Hall, he should really be called, Lazarus!' I suppose there was an element of truth in what he was saying. John really had been so close to death that it did seem like he'd been literally raised from the dead. The meaning of the promise the Lord had given me several months before was now becoming crystal clear. 'I'll give you back a healthy child.' Now like a jigsaw puzzle we were able to piece that promise together. On reflection, it felt as though John had been taken away from us completely during his time in Intensive Care, before he had been miraculously given back. When I later asked Dr Rylance why he compared John to Lazarus he explained that when he saw John appear through his office door he suddenly felt, 'The cheek of him, he shouldn't be here!' He knew what state John's brain was in and felt that there was no way he should have made it. But John was large as life and bringing us a tremendous amount of pleasure.

One evening, not long after John was discharged from hospital, as I was holding him in his bath he looked up and said, 'Light.' As I gazed at his little face I noticed just how bright and shiny his eyes were. Immediately I squealed with gratitude, 'Thank God for his shining eyes!' Dave obviously heard me from the bedroom and called back 'Amen!' We were so grateful to have John, and not only that, but to have him looking so healthy. Many parents can never reach that level of deep appreciation for the life of a child for they've never faced his or her imminent death. We would never have known such love if we'd never known such agony. If one good thing had come out of all the suffering, it was deep, deep gratitude.

Term had finished while John was still in Intensive Care, and many students who had completed their training had gone off to their respective churches to take up posts as Probationary Ministers. However, having become so involved with John, they were keen to have an update on his condition. We often received calls and letters enquiring after him. Something of the Spirit of God stirred inside me one day when a note arrived from one such student who was pleased to hear through the grapevine just how well John was doing. Her prayer was that God would pour His love and His strength into John's life to make up for the lost time. She qualified this by quoting Joel 2:25 which reads: I will repay you for the years the locusts have eaten.

When I found the verse I knew instantly the promise was for John. In a way it was an assurance that the Lord still had John in His care; that He had not forgotten him and, indeed, He had everything in hand. This latest promise was another to add to the promises we'd already been given:

1. I will not let your foot slip
2. I'll give you back a healthy child
3. Save the son of your handmaiden
4. This is John, strong and bright and unflickering
5. With long life will I satisfy you.

To feel the living God communicating through the words of a friend and through the Scriptures filled us with the most wonderful feeling of peace and expectation. The locusts certainly had eaten into our son but nothing is too difficult for the Lord Jesus Christ to put right. Over the following months we were to see a restoration slowly take place in John.

142

Holiday in Paignton in August

After the trauma of the past few months we were desperate for a holiday; one which would help to consolidate us as a family. With the disappointment of Jersey still fresh in our minds we were a little apprehensive to say the least, but we went ahead anyway and booked a fortnight's stay in a guest-house in Paignton.

With six bodies plus too much luggage packed tightly into and onto the car, the drive to Paignton developed into a typical 'Hall' journey. We passed the time in our usual manner; community singing, with, 'We're all going on a summer holiday,' surpassing the others. (Eat your heart out, Cliff!) We chatted about everything under the sun and listened to favourite cassettes whilst munching and nibbling, and obviously drinking too much because every now and again we had to cover our ears when an irritated Dave shouted, 'Hold it in, I'm definitely not stopping for the toilet again!'

When we eventually approached our destination we did the 'Best behaviour at the Guest House' routine and gave the children a resume of what we intended to do on arrival. I started to explain that we would unpack our clothes and put them in the drawers, when suddenly to our surprise young David burst out crying and sobbed uncontrollably. 'David, whatever is the matter?' we asked. It took a little while for him to dry his tears before we eventually got to the root of the problem. 'I don't want anyone to draw on my clothes!' he wailed. We were all in fits of laughter as we explained that the 'drawers' we were referring to were not people!

The holiday was marvellous and did us all the world

of good, although it took several days before we fully unwound. It wasn't until we were nearing the end of the holiday that we realised just how uptight we had all been. The past year had taken its toll. The children adored the beach, especially John whose favourite occupation was eating sand and crunching shells! It was exhausting constantly trying to clean out his mouth and pick shells from his teeth, but I often felt like nipping myself to see if this was all real and not a dream. Only a couple of months before he was at death's door, and now he was on the beach having the time of his life!

It was during the holiday that John took his first few steps, only eight weeks after surgery. Mind you, we were so crushed in the Guest House bedroom that he had very little option but to walk since there was no room to fall down! Yet it was progress and we were thrilled considering that after his surgery there had been the possibility of a right-sided paralysis. We were eager to share the good news with his physiotherapist and, indeed, to all who were involved with John's development.

We had to pass each day a little hotel, with brightly lit fairy lights, that looked so warm, clean and inviting to me. Caroline overheard me commenting to Dave on how much I'd love to stay in a hotel like that since it had a dance floor, bar and a warm friendly atmosphere. The following day she shouted, 'Mum, look at that hotel over there, you'd love it, it's got a BAR!' Dave and I collapsed with laughter and immediately tried to explain, in a whisper, that it wasn't the kind of thing a future minister's wife should be dreaming of, and her daughter shouting about!

We returned from our holiday refreshed and felt ready to face life again. What we would once have considered an emergency now felt quite insignificant.

One day, for example, when I had my head buried in work, Dave came into the room and asked me to have a look at one of his toes. He'd stubbed it earlier, whilst kicking the ball around with young David. I glanced over at a rather discoloured, swollen, tender-looking toe that he was unable to bend, and informed him in an almost monotone voice that he'd broken it. I put my head down and carried on with what I was doing and Dave hobbled out of the room.

A few moments later I burst out laughing when it occurred to me just how callous I had sounded. Dave returned to the room, intrigued to find out what was amusing me. 'Dave, some people rush off to casualty with broken toes and here I am dismissing yours with not even as much as an ounce of sympathy or advice! Take some gauze and tape and strap two toes together,' I advised him. 'The adjacent toe acts as a splint. That's all they would do for you in casualty anyway.' (Providing treatments hadn't changed much since I was a casualty nurse!)

Another little episode springs to mind. It happened early one morning when we awoke to the sound of water splashing in our bedroom. We immediately thought that one of the children was mistaking our bedroom for the toilet. (This had happened before when one of them was half-asleep; the kitchen floor being the target!) However, after switching on the bedside light the problem was revealed. Water was literally pouring through the ceiling and down the light fitments onto our bed. Any other couple, alarmed, would have contacted the college caretaker straightaway to inform him of the emergency. Not us, we simply pushed the bed over; aligned a baby bath under the flow; didn't bother changing the wet sheets but moved to the dry side of the bed and with the gentle sound of flood waters, fell fast asleep! We had no idea how much water was pooling above and were not daunted by the possibility that the ceiling could cave in at any minute! We didn't see any point in looking for bridges to cross. Since John's illness we had started to see life's little hassles in a less irritating light.

Child Development Centre
John was referred to the Child Development Centre at the Children's Hospital, where he was assessed over a period of several weeks, and a recommendation made for him to attend the nursery class there for two days a week. The input was excellent and included physio-therapy, speech therapy, occupational therapy and a teacher. There was a nursery nurse and helpers on hand as well as a health visitor and psychologist. We could not have asked for better support and expertise.

Extra classes were run and I was invited to attend with John. I was always the first to admit if he was incapable of some particular task but quite often, after watching him fail even the simplest test, I would feel demoralised and near to tears. The staff were wonderful and often reminded me just what he'd been through. What I admired most was their perseverance and pa-tience as well as their ability never to give up. This eventually paid off when John showed signs of finally grasping the fact that the 'round' shape fitted the round hole and not the square!

He loved the music sessions especially, but although he knew the words to most of the songs and could sing them, he did not have the ability to sing along with the others. If we started he would stop, but he could be heard singing the current rhymes at random by himself later. It seemed as though he had difficulty concentrating on the two areas at the same time.

Physically by this time he was running around and very rarely walked. He ran on his toes with his chest sticking out and his arms flung back giving the impression that he was impersonating an aeroplane. He adopted this posture to help his balance, which was so poor that at times he would fall down for no apparent reason. He was measured for a safety helmet which eased the burden of trying to protect him.

One day, I was watching John from the window as he 'flew' around the college grounds with Dave chasing him. He fell many times but just laughed and picked himself up. He loved to be out and about and to play with the other children, and never seemed to notice that he was any different from them. Momentarily, as I watched him, it was almost as if life stood still and everything in the past was a blur. 'Had I dreamed the last few months or had all of it actually happened? Was that really John, my son, out there so disabled?' Every movement he made looked such an effort and gave the impression that he had to expend a terrible amount of energy as he struggled to hobble around. 'Why am I standing here crying?' His giggles had reached my ears and made me snap out of self-pity. He had no concept of what he'd been through in the past and was just bursting with the joy of living. John was living for the day, for the moment, and was so full of happiness and fun it was infectious.

I reminded myself firstly that things could quite easily have gone the other way and that we might not have him with us at all, and secondly that many mothers with children confined to wheelchairs would do anything to see their child running around. Hadn't I made a pact with the Lord that I would be content if He brought John round enough to know who we were? He knew who we were alright, but not only that, here he was talking, walking and understanding. Wasn't that an unexpected bonus? How dare I be so ungrateful!

Christmas seemed to be upon us before we knew it. The excitement was mounting in our household for the arrival of Santa. John knew Santa's picture and could say his name but he was unaware of what he represented and that presents would await him on Christmas morning. When it was feared that we would lose him I often imagined what Christmas would be like without him and couldn't bear the thought of waking on Christmas morning and John not being there to share in the excitement with the family.

Dave and I were Christmas shopping one afternoon and, after fighting our way through the crowds, we came to a standstill outside a huge store. I thought of the parents who had lost children that year and who would have no children to buy presents for this Christmas. The burden of sadness was so great that I stood staring into the shop window with tears stinging my eyes. Dave sensed what I was thinking and we shared how awful it must be for families at this time who had lost their precious son or daughter, and in a way how awkward it was for us to identify with them since John's life had been spared.

In the past when something troubled me it always helped to write about it in prose or poetry. It was getting it off my chest. That day I needed to do just that and immediately put pen to paper:

> The shops are bursting with Christmas wealth
> on this last day of October,
> Children's faces radiant
> as they squeeze through endless crowds
> enthralled by this year's 'big stores' window show.
> Santa's party and snowmen nodding heads
> as toy soldiers beat drums
> in time to familiar festive melodies.
> Victorian children's mouths open and close
> as their carol books, covered in snow, move rhythmically
> to complete this authentic looking scene.
> Rays from coloured lights radiate a warmth to shoppers and
> challenge the dusk.
>
> As I meditate on what's represented here,
> I reflect on the pain we recently shared.
>
> We would have changed it if we could,
> Stopped the suffering there and then,
> But evidently helpless ...

We cried; we prayed; we loved; we watched and waited;
Each comforting the other, heartbroken, bonded in our grief,
Would the sadness and emptiness ever go away?
We wondered ...

Tears sting my eyes as I'm jostled by the crowd,
Tears of compassion,

'Oh God help you this Christmastime'

Our children dreadfully ill,

But my child lived ...

E. Hall Nov 92

Throughout life we all continually face problems and fears as disappointments, broken relationships or bereavements come our way. Never before had I experienced anything to compare with the agony John's illness had brought, and yet my pain would be no more intense than the pain felt by the seventeen year old whose heart is broken in love. How can you quickly mature the child with the broken toy? We each need to see our problems through, however small or seemingly great they appear to be.

But there were moments by John's bedside when this felt increasingly more difficult to do. With plenty of time to think, I often reflected on my past and longed for my single days again, 'flatting' as we called it, in London. The good old days or so we like to believe. Problems then? I thought I had, but really the only one was deciding which boyfriend I was in love with at the time! Irritations? Yes, having to leave the dance floor at 3 am when we would've danced till dawn! My reminiscing only served to highlight a need to escape from reality, away from the present, away from responsibility, away from the uncertainty of it all, just for a little while.

One thing to be grateful for was the fact that I had been able to look at John as he lay unconscious in front of me and know that I had no past regrets. Like most other mothers after their children are born, the choice was there for me to either return to work or to stay at home and be a full-time mother. I chose to do the latter and, despite missing my career at times and struggling financially, for me personally, I had made the right decision. I had given him my best, my all.

CHAPTER 13

STATIONING
(1st January-7th May 1993)

By the turn of the year excitement was mounting among the students who were due to leave college in the summer. A committee responsible for placing students in the appropriate churches met at Queens to carry out that unenviable task. Each student had previously filled out a questionnaire telling a little about themselves and stating any sound reasons why it would be helpful for them to be placed in a particular area e.g. dependent parents. They had also to mention a geographical point where they would like to serve the Lord and if they had any preference for rural, suburban or inner city areas. Dave requested somewhere between Glasgow and Newcastle for obvious reasons.

When D day (19th January) arrived, the applicants had to line up outside the tutor's office, a few at a time in alphabetical order. The married students brought their spouses so that they would receive the news together. There was such buzz and excitement around the college. Throughout the morning, coffee was served in front of an open fire in the 'common-room' and it was certainly appreciated, especially by those whose surname began with Z! Those returning from the tutor's office, flushed and clutching details of their new placement, welcomed a drink and the opportunity to share their news.

It occurred to me as we waited patiently to be called that it was similar to lining up to see the school nurse! It was a bit much when we started acting like school children, chattering and giggling and making inappropriate comments such as, 'What if we get sent to the Shetlands?' or 'What if they've lost my file?' As each student appeared from the office they were swamped by bodies with only one question, 'Where are you going?'

When our turn came, we couldn't straighten out the nervous grin fixed on our faces as we sat down in the tutor's office. He was retrieving our folder from under a pile of papers, 'Where do you think you're going?' Dave took a guess at Carlisle or Darlington. 'No, you're not going there. Have you heard of a place called East Kilbride?' *EAST KILBRIDE?* Had we heard of it? It was only about ten miles from where we used to live, I had relatives there! It was a gift. It was going home. The pluses for being stationed there were many:

1. John would be transferred back to Dr Stephenson in Glasgow, saving us from having to start afresh at another hospital.

2. I had secretly hoped we would be given one church to look after as in Methodism it's not uncommon to have three or four or more churches. I got my wish!

3. We would be back near family and friends again, and (who would have believed it?) my cousin who was storing our piano lived in East Kilbride!

4. John would miss the Scottish school intake by a couple of months which would give us another year for him to try and catch up with his development.

It was wonderful sharing the news with our parents over the phone - they were so thrilled, as were our colleagues when we joined them in the common-room amidst the din. We had approximately seven months to prepare ourselves mentally for the move and to make the necessary practical arrangements. Like us, the children were desperate to see the church and manse, so a few weeks later we journeyed up north to do just that and to meet the congregation. The visit went well, with no complaints from us or the children. From then on it seemed only part of us was in Birmingham and the other part was mentally preparing for our new life in Scotland.

At times I wondered if I would indeed be 'ready' when the time would come for us to move. Serious illness with its after-effects and moving house, considered two of the most stressful situations, were about to join hands and I honestly wondered if I would be able to handle the combination of both. The old cliche, 'Stop the world, I want to get off', was starting to mean more to me than it had ever done in the past. Evidence of this pressure came in subtle little ways, for instance on the day when our tempers flared over a simple misunderstanding.

We had an early morning appointment for John to have plasters applied to his legs in the hope that the treatment would improve his walking. Our home is always in a guddle in the morning and we constantly run late, and of course love, peace, patience, kindness and gentleness tend to give way to shouting, tempers, frustration, arguments and fall outs! This particular morning was no exception but I intended, despite the storm, to be on time for the appointment. We planned to drop the children off at school on the way to the hospital so I offered to take a neighbour's little lad to school since we had to go anyway. Fortunately for the boy she declined, because what ensued could only be described as complete and utter downright childish behaviour of the hysterical variety.

The problem arose from poor communication - at the best of times our brains aren't in top gear but in the mornings we would need a jump-start. Dave was under the impression I was asking our neighbour to take our children to school, allowing us to drive straight to the hospital as we were running a little late. So when our children piled into the car, followed by my explanation, he erupted. As Dave drove, we continued to shout and argue, each one convinced the other was wrong. This was not just a simple argument, this was Guinness Book of Records material. Of course the disagreement ran its usual course with me digging up the past by screaming, 'May I remind you, Mr Hall, it's your fault we're down here in the first place!' The real feelings of Mrs Hall were certainly out in the open now. It made a nonsense of my promises to support Dave totally as he trained for the ministry, wiping out my noblest intentions in a matter of seconds.

I was aware as we verbally battered each other that Dave's driving was becoming faster and more erratic. Then, to my horror, as we came to a T-junction to turn left, instead of sitting patiently behind the cars waiting to turn right, he drove down the left-hand side of them, mounting the kerb as he went along, with the car screeching Stirling Moss style. When he slowed down at the junction I screamed, 'Stop the car! Let me out! I just hope there's a policeman around and if he hasn't managed to get your number, I'll give him it! In fact if you end up in court I'll go as a witness for the prosecution!' Such was my rage.

Our poor children were in the back of the car terrified. We very rarely have rows and it was for this reason the children were so taken aback. I was full of remorse when Caroline got out of the car crying. Louise and David looked too shocked to say a thing. What an atmosphere in which to leave them at school. I continued to rant and rave until we reached the hospital and didn't even say goodbye to Dave when he dropped me off.

Of course, my attitude changed completely on arriving at Outpatients where I was as sweet as honey to everyone in sight, although to be truthful I was very shaken by the pathetic episode. When Dave and I met again, several hours after we'd had a chance to calm down, we were able to sort out the misunderstanding and felt rather stupid for the morning's drama. Have you been there?

I shall never forget, however, the look on Caroline's face when I collected the children from school that afternoon. She looked up into my face and asked desperately, 'Where's Dad?' I put my arm around her, 'He's at home, I came for a walk.'

'Oh, I thought he was in prison.' She sounded so relieved. Bless her, she had been worrying all day. I said how sorry I was for what had happened as we walked home together and continued to explain that we don't like it either when they fight with each other. (A rather poor attempt to justify our intolerable behaviour!)

I'm not very tall but I was certainly cut down to size when Caroline innocently informed me: 'And anyway Mum, it wasn't Dad who brought us down here, God sent us.' Talk about 'out of the mouths of babes'; how humbling. Firmly put in my place by my daughter, I was reminded that we were indeed answering a 'call' and no protests from me could ever change that truth.

The College Healing Service

Dave, Louise and I were invited to take part in a drama, *Jairus' Daughter*, which was to be performed in the college chapel during a healing service at the beginning of February. I was especially keen to be involved since I had missed so much of college life in our first year, with John being so ill. It was a very moving play and touched the hearts of many in the congregation.

Louise played Jairus' daughter and we, her parents. Dave had to enter carrying Louise, appearing dead, in his arms and place her at my feet, where I had to weep over her. During a song, as 'Christ' raised Louise (whose acting was superb for a child of her age) 'from the dead,' I looked up at Dave and saw tears brimming in his eyes. It was then I realised the play was a little too near the bone for him and served to bring it all home again. The thought had passed my mind that we had, in real life, been in a similar situation to the one portrayed in the play. Yet because it was Louise lying at our feet and not John, I couldn't feel the same emotion as Dave was obviously experiencing.

Many colleagues, some of them red-eyed, later shared how they admired us for our contribution to the service and how difficult it must have been to perform that particular play. It was a privilege to be in the company of such genuine and caring people.

A Setback

About a week later we had a bad start to the week when on Monday morning I discovered that one of the goldfish had jumped out of the bowl to its death! My first impression when I saw only one fish swimming in the water was that one had eaten the other. But there on the floor lay a rather hairy looking goldfish. It had obviously wriggled around on the carpet acquiring fluff and dirt as it struggled to survive. Poor thing. 'Is it Annabel or Goldie?' Caroline sobbed. They both looked identical to me; I hadn't a clue as I'd shown very little interest in the two goldfish I'd never wanted in the first place! But we promised Caroline we'd buy another from the pet shop and fit a safety net to the bowl to prevent a repeat performance!

On Monday afternoon the School Secretary rang asking for Louise to be taken home as she'd had a nasty bang to her head. The school photographs were being taken the following morning so we were hoping the 'egg' wasn't in a prominent position! Fortunately, she was none the worse for the accident, although the rather enormous looking bump at the side of her head was extremely tender to touch. She curled up on a chair, thumb in her mouth and slept for the rest of the afternoon.

My GP had arranged for me to have an ECG at the local hospital the following morning as I had been complaining of chest pains. After the test, I rushed down to the school with the boys for the photographic session which only served to remind us that one shouldn't work with animals or children! Then, after dropping us home, Dave drove off to pick up a friend for whom he'd promised to do a favour. An hour or so later he appeared through the door, pale and subdued, and, in that 'I'd suppose I better tell her' guilty type voice, announced, 'I've just smashed into a Mercedes.' That 'What next?' 'sinking' 'tell me it isn't true' feeling came over me before I accused him, in my ever-loving, sympathetic, high-pitched voice, 'You couldn't have been paying attention; you obviously weren't watching where you were going; your head's always in the clouds.' No one was injured fortunately, which was really all that mattered, but it was starting to feel like it was going to be one of those weeks.

Just to add to it all, on Wednesday my GP informed me that the ECG result had shown 'changes' so she was sending me to see a cardiologist. Personally at that point, I felt it was more like a psychiatrist I needed to see!

One dead goldfish;

One bang to the head;

One car accident;

and one doubtful heart before the final crunch.

On Friday afternoon John came home from the hospital nursery as right as rain, but a short while later Dave found him lying on the floor in the hall in a grand mal fit. My mind was swirling. 'Can it be starting all over again?' He'd had seven clear months and was doing extremely well. After a double dose of Valium rectally he was still convulsing so we were forced to call an ambulance. Dr Mitchell was ready and waiting in casualty with the appropriate treatment. We appreciated the fact that the doctors knew John so well which saved us from going into his history at great length. John was eventually admitted to Ward 6.

It turned out his temperature was high and this had obviously triggered off the convulsion but, much to our relief, he remained fit free for the couple of days in the ward, despite there being difficulty in bringing his temperature down. We were relieved that this appeared to be an isolated incident. It was good to see familiar faces again in one respect, but we felt deeply for these children whose lives revolve around hospital wards.

Another consequence was attending the funerals of fellow patients who eventually lose their fight for life. One such child was little Carrie Anne who at the tender age of two went to be with her Creator. Her funeral was very moving and was well attended by friends and staff from the hospital. It served to bring home to us that it could just as easily have been John. Our year with him had been rough, and helping him to recover now was hard work, but as parents our suffering in comparison to others had been minimal. For some children, hospital becomes their second home with an alternating pattern of a few weeks with their family, then back to the ward for treatment. We only had a taste of that routine but for them that lifestyle is the norm.

160

It did us good to see the staff of Ward 6 again and catch up with all their news; one married, a few expecting babies, one or two promotions and so on. They were so delighted, despite this little setback, that John was doing well. They had been through so much with us in the past that we viewed them more like friends than hospital staff. When John left the ward we promised to pop in every now and again before we finally left for Scotland.

With the goldfish now replaced; the bump on Louise's head much flatter; the car accident in the hands of the insurers and John back to his old self, there was only one problem left to sort out. Me!

The Cardiologist arranged for me to have a 'Stress ECG' at a neighbouring hospital. This entailed walking on a treadmill for several minutes whilst a tracing of the heart function was recorded simultaneously on an ECG monitor. I had absolutely no pain during this procedure and had in fact felt I was wasting their time. When the test was finished, however, the doctor officiating explained that the chest pains I had had were due to a condition known as angina and commenced me on medication straightaway. I was completely shocked at this result and walked home from the hospital in disbelief. With none of the predisposing factors for coronary artery disease, other than hereditary, how can I possibly have angina?

The chest pains and tiredness continued and basically I managed to struggle through each day; some days feeling much better than others. One day, to my amusement, a neighbour at college shared a conversation she'd had with Caroline when she was enquiring after me.

'Well,' Caroline replied, 'She's got this thing called ANGINA*S* but it can't be very bad because it hasn't stopped her talking!' I knew I would live! Children have such a unique way of bringing problems into the right perspective.

Louise was in the wars again! Yet another bang on the head but this time she showed definite head injury symptoms which, under GP orders, resulted in a visit to casualty and a subsequent admission to the children's ward of Selly Oak Hospital. Our family was certainly getting round the Birmingham hospitals in our short stay there! Louise was extremely drowsy and felt very sick as we waited patiently for the X-ray films to be developed. It was during our wait in the X-ray department that I got talking to a young mother who was attending with her two year old son.

She had appeared pushing her son on a trolley and came over to wait beside us. We chatted to pass the time, as most patients in hospital waiting areas do. She commented on how poorly Louise looked, then proceeded to share with me the problems she'd been having with her son. Apparently he'd just had a convulsion which was the result of a high temperature. She seemed quite agitated and nervous which is understandable after what she'd just been through, but her little son was jumping around on the trolley obviously well recovered from the ordeal and unaware of the upset he'd just caused.

Then came the remark which put a kind of wry smile on my face. 'You know that's the third convulsion he's had in two years.' John could have three fits in two minutes! And probably in a year he had an estimated one thousand. I opened my mouth to assure her that from personal experience I could identify fully with what she was going through, but instead simply paused momentarily before offering some sympathy, 'Oh dear, how awful. I'm sure he'll be fine.'

Louise recovered well and was discharged the following morning.

CHAPTER 14

EPILOGUE

I had mixed emotions as the time drew near for us to return to Scotland. I had never imagined that I would feel so confused. It was probably for the best that I didn't have a choice in the matter. Although in saying that, several months before we had in actual fact been presented with a choice. It was felt we needed time to consolidate as a family after our ordeal over the past year, so we were given the option to stay on at college for a further year. After weighing up the pros and cons we decided it would be better for us as a family all round if we declined the offer. But during the upheaval, amidst the guddle, as I packed boxes only to discover John emptying them as soon as my back was turned, it occurred to me that perhaps the option to stay on at college hadn't been such a pointless suggestion after all.

Dave was looking forward to the move and was keen to get settled down in East Kilbride and start his work as a probationer minister at St Andrew's Methodist Church. Louise, David and John were nonchalant, but poor Caroline was absolutely heartbroken when the day finally arrived for us to say goodbye to our friends in Birmingham. The fact that other families were also leaving brought her very little comfort. As a minister's daughter, moving every few years was something she would need to try to get used to, at least until she was at an independent age. No doubt the older our children get, the harder it is going to be for them.

The months of August and September were extremely busy months, unpacking the boxes, meeting the congregation and settling the children into their new schools. Before long, however, we were able to draw our breath and concentrate our energies on finding John a place at a suitable nursery school. This search was intensified when on one particular day, to our horror John opened our front door, escaped down an embankment and on to a busy road where he was almost hit by a bus. Two members of our congregation (who must be part-time angels!) were on the bus, recognised John and brought him safely home. John appeared through the front door smiling and totally unaware of the danger he'd been in. To have gone through so much with John only to have him killed outright in a matter of seconds would have been unbearable.

The psychologist recommended Craighead Nursery School in Blantyre which catered for children with special needs. John has been a pupil there now for several months. All the expert care he was given at the Child Development Centre in Birmingham continues in this nursery. He absolutely adores his time spent there three days a week and for us the blessing has been in seeing the steady progress in his development.

His speech has improved dramatically; he uses more sentences now and answers questions much more appropriately. Nevertheless, normal conversation is still lacking - something of John seems locked away somewhere. He wears day-time splints which have improved his walking and balance and for the first time in his life he is able to go up and down stairs by himself, gripping tight to the hand rail with supervision. John hasn't lost his healthy appetite, nor his remarkable good nature, nor his love for music. He feeds himself and is fully toilet-trained.

Some of the simplest of tasks John finds difficult to perform such as children's easy jigsaw puzzles or drawing or copying anything recognisable; he can only scribble with a pen and seems unable to join in any constructive or imaginative play (much to his brother's dismay). He does know colours and shapes (even hexagons!) and can recognise numbers written in any order from 1-100. At three and a half years old he was able to read sentences constructed from words I had taught him together with words he had learned from his brother's reading book. It appears that certain areas of John's brain are developing normally whilst other parts are quite delayed; but the heartening fact is he's still progressing.

Although he hasn't remained completely fit free, we can handle the odd fit now and again in the *hope* that one day they will eventually stop.

Hope is a precious fruit that I've been able to eat afresh since John's illness, tasting its sweetness as if for the first time. It has been said, 'Where there's life, there's hope.' True, but when all hope appears lost, and that cliche loses its punch, there is still the hope in Jesus. It would seem after our miracle that I would find it easier now to pray for a miracle for others in need, but strangely enough this was not so initially. We had indeed encountered heaven, albeit with our mind's eye, but when God opens up a little glimpse of the heavenly realms, a tiny peep at that new and wonderful dimension, it makes praying for healing so much more difficult. As Paul writes, 'For me to live is Christ, to die is gain' (Philippians 1:21).

Dave's ministry has certainly been enriched by the experience of the past few years. Suffering dissolves some of the shallowness in our natures and helps us identify more with others. This has been brought home to Dave during his role as pastor of the congregation where he finds himself sharing in the hurts and pains of men and women. It has been particularly helpful when talking with newly bereaved families, as well as those who need prayers for healing. He is able to draw from past experience and share how he felt in the midst of our trauma, testifying to the fact of God's daily grace being sufficient for us. Many become angry, confused and even bitter towards God when in distress, but through this helpless honesty the Spirit comes and breathes His peace. It is perhaps the greatest privilege of ministry to be allowed to share the deeply personal sufferings of others and to prayerfully walk alongside them through their trials.

Our children seem to have suffered no ill effects as a result of what John's illness brought to us as a family and have a unique love for their little brother. Perhaps young David needs a little more reassurance than the girls do, because with John being so demanding at times it is so easy to see how the others could be pushed aside. Therefore, as often as we possibly can, we make a conscious effort each day to take time with them as individuals.

A lot of water has gone under the bridge since John's first convulsion; but thankfully we've been kept from drowning. It would appear that God's promise, *I'll give you back a healthy child*, has not been fulfilled since John is still subject to fits periodically, there is a delay in his development and he is not fully able-bodied. Yet we honestly believe that promise is slowly being realised with each new day.

I don't suppose he has any recollection of the two years spent in Birmingham or remembers the people to whom we owe so much and have grown to love and admire. Perhaps one day, when he's older, we could introduce him to them all over again. The many friends at Queen's and the staff and children in the hospital will always have a special place in our hearts.

I find it hard to think of the children we met and loved on Ward 6 without some element of heartache filtering through. Some of them still struggling on in their illness, accepting it very well, and despite 'off days' radiating a brave inner beauty. The others who lost their fight for life; I think of Carrie Anne, I think of Steven, I think of Natasha, I think of James, I think of Angela, I think of Toni and I think of Billy...

I dedicate this book to them with fondest love.

GLOSSARY

INVESTIGATIONS

CAT SCAN

Computerised Axial Tomography. A series of narrow x-ray beams is passed through a cross section of the body or brain at different angles and levels. The information is detected by a machine called a scintillator which feeds into the computer the density of tissue the x-rays have passed through. The computer processes this information and produces a 3 dimensional image. Individual slices ranging from 1.5 mm-13 mm can also be selected and studied on the screen or copied on film for permanent study. CT Scans are precise in measuring differences in density, i.e. high density tissue (bone) appears white, whilst low density (air, liquids) appear black; in between, organs and tissues appear grey. Tumours, cysts, blood clots and haemorrhages of the brain can be identified.

MRI SCAN

Magnetic Resonance Imaging works under the principle that water molecules (nerve cells have a high hydrogen-rich water content) absorb a magnetic field, so instead of x-rays or isotopes, a powerful circular magnet is used to detect radiowaves displayed by a television monitor. MRI has the advantage of not having the problem of visual 'noise' interference which can occur in CT scans so therefore very high quality three dimensional pictures can be built up to show quite clearly the grey and white brain matter and different types of tissue. It identifies scarring in the brain more readily than CT or SPECT. Scans and shows much better contrast in soft tissue especially allowing better sensitivity for the detection of tumours and blood clots.

SPECT SCAN

Single Photon Emission Computerised Tomography. Where CT Scan describes regional *structure* of the anatomy, SPECT measures regional *function*, usually as blood flow to muscle, heart and more particularly to the brain. Any part of brain tissue involved in a seizure requires more oxygen and sugar and therefore the blood flow is increased to meet the demand. By injecting a radioactive isotope during a seizure, a chemical attached to the isotope distributes it in the same pattern as blood flow and the pattern is fixed, highlighting those areas of the brain involved in the seizure. The computer analyses the information received and produces a three dimensional picture of the brain.

EEG

Electroencephalograph is a machine which records the electrical activity of the brain. The EEG picks up the electrical impulses from various areas of the surface of the brain simultaneously, amplifies and records them on a moving paper roll. EEG's are used to support a clinical diagnosis of e.g. epilepsy or cerebral tumour, but cannot be relied on solely since healthy people can show abnormal tracings at times.

LUMBAR PUNCTURE

is the name given to the process by which a specimen of cerebro-spinal fluid which circulates around the brain and spinal cord is obtained. This can be done by introducing a special lumbar puncture needle between the spines of the 3rd and 4th lumbar vertebrae. The specimen is extremely useful in diagnosing some neurological conditions such as tumours, blood clots, or haemorrhages of the brain and meningitis in its various forms.

DRUGS

MMR VACCINE
Measles, Mumps and Rubella (German measles) triple vaccine has replaced the original measles vaccination and can be given any time after the age of 12 months although it is more commonly given around the 15 month stage. It would normally be withheld if the child was showing acute febrile symptoms; or if for any reason his/her immunity was lowered; if allergies, particularly to egg have been identified or in the case of a female adult where pregnancy is suspected.

HEMINEVRIN (Chlormethiazole)
This drug is used orally in capsule or syrup form as a sedative and in withdrawal symptoms in alcoholism. It is also used intravenously to control status epilepticus and pre-eclamptic toxaemia in pregnancy. There is no antidote for this drug.

DIAZEPAM
is from the benzodiazepine family and has many uses. It is effective as a sedative; is a muscle relaxant; reduces anxiety and has anti-convulsant properties. It is used in status epilepticus intra-venously or rectally.

MIDAZOLAM
(Hypnovel) is a benzodiazepine given intra-muscularly or intravenously to induce sleep during minor surgical procedures. It is often used to reduce anxiety and as a muscle relaxant and has anti-convulsant properties.

FLUMAZENIL
is a benzodiazepine antagonist. It is used to reverse the central sedative effects of benzodiazepines during anaesthesia or in ICU.

STEROIDS
Synthetically prepared hormones which have anti-inflammatory properties. They are often effective in reducing oedema (fluid in the tissues) of the brain.

THIOPENTONE
when given intra-venously produces general anaesthesia and can also be used for the control of convulsive states.

ANTI-CONVULSANTS
A group of drugs prescribed to prevent or arrest convulsions.

TPN
Total Parental Nutrition is an alternative form of feeding when food cannot be ingested or tolerated enterally. Nutrients can be given through a peripheral vein but because the vessels become irritated over a prolonged period, a major central vessel is usually preferred for long-term feeding. A larger vein is selected from the scalp, elbow, ankle or neck and a long line inserted through this vein until it reaches the top right chamber of the heart (atrium). The feed is delivered through a 'drip' into this long line and therefore into the systemic circulation. TPN is prepared under the strictest sterile conditions to meet the daily needs of the individual and involves the expertise of personnel in the pharmacy, dietetics and biochemistry departments.

MEDICAL CONDITIONS

GRAND MAL FIT
Many describe an aura or strange sensation prior to a fit, then consciousness is lost and they fall to the ground. Initially all muscles go into spasm and this rigidity (tonic stage) is followed by jerking movements of face and limbs (clonic stage) before a deep sleep ensues.

STATUS EPILEPTICUS

A medical emergency occurs when one fit succeeds the next one without consciousness being regained. It is vital that these attacks are controlled as soon as possible because if they are allowed to continue for more than half an hour it becomes potentially dangerous as this can cause serious damage to the brain or even be fatal.

CORTICAL DYSPLASIA

is a very rare congenital disorder where a part of the cortex or gray matter which is distributed mainly around the outside of the brain develops abnormally. Instead of the normal smooth convolutions, the affected area can be unusually tough and misshapen. These areas can give rise to seizures.

ENCEPHALITIS

is an inflammation of the brain usually caused by a viral infection. The brain substance only may be affected or the coverings of the brain (meninges) may also be involved. The herpes simplex virus (the same virus which causes the common cold sore) most frequently causes encephalitis although other viral conditions such as mumps and measles can also give rise to the condition. Depending on the severity, symptoms may be so mild that they are hardly noticed or may range from anything from headache, fever, mental disturbance, seizures, paralysis, loss of consciousness and coma. Whilst some patients recover completely others may be left with brain injury, behavioural disturbances or epilepsy.

MEDICAL PROCEDURE

INTUBATION

A special tube is introduced into the air passages to allow air to enter the lungs. This is done following the administration of a drug which paralyses all muscles including respiratory. The tube is then connected to a ventilator.